First American Ambassador to Guinea

JOHN H. MORROW

RUTGERS UNIVERSITY PRESS

New Brunswick   New Jersey

To Rowena, Jean, and John

ACKNOWLEDGMENT

My wife, daughter, and son have contributed much toward the completion of this book with ideas, suggestions, and encouragement; but more important were their love, devotion, tireless help, and sacrifices without which I could not have withstood the rigorous demands of the tour of duty in Guinea. I am indebted to Kathleen Jones for invaluable aid in typing the manuscript. A special word is due my colleagues in the Foreign Service whose loyalty and dedication enabled me to carry on in Guinea.

J. H. M.

Introduction

As I made my way through the winding streets of Paris toward the Quai d'Orsay during the hot summer of 1958, I had no way of knowing that the events of that summer would change my way of life and catapult me, a Negro college professor teaching in North Carolina, into the realm of diplomacy. Supposedly, I was en route to Algeria and French West Africa, where I hoped to get additional data for a manuscript on challenge and response in French colonial politics. But in Paris I was experiencing setback after setback in my effort to convince the French authorities that I should be allowed to continue to Algeria. The French Army had staged an uprising in Algeria in May 1958, and conditions there were still very unsettled and certainly unsafe for civilian travel.

I had made an appointment with an official at the Quai d'Orsay in the hope that he might be of some assistance to me in securing passage to North Africa. Although the official showed polite interest in my desire to get to Algeria, he reminded me that the city of Algiers was no longer in civilian hands but under military control. He asked me whether I had attended the colloquium held the previous summer at the

University of Manchester. I told him I had never been in England. He asked me whether any of my recent articles had been discussed at this conference. I told him I doubted very much that anybody at such a gathering would have any interest in anything I had written. The Frenchman pulled out from among the papers on his desk a reprint of an article that I had written in 1955 entitled "Unrest in North Africa." At this moment I realized that I would never obtain passage to Algeria, for in the article I had suggested that the French should get out of Algeria, a proposal diametrically opposed to the prevailing sentiment in 1958, which sought to keep the French in Algeria at any cost.

I am indebted to William Witman II, then serving as First Secretary of the Embassy and Officer in Charge of African Affairs, and his very able assistant, young David Korn, for their suggestion that I might profitably spend my time in Paris talking with African students and officials who were spending the summer there, and also with important officials at the French Overseas Ministry. I believe that those conversations with the Africans and the French during that vexatious summer had something to do with my subsequent appointment as the first American Ambassador to the Republic of Guinea the following June.

The conversations with the officials at the French Overseas Ministry were stimulating because we discussed primarily the subject of African independence. I was struck by the readiness with which each of these men, all of whom had spent years in the colonial service, talked about the right of French territories to independence. They saw independence, however, as coming only after an evolutionary period during which these territories would be prepared to assume the responsibilities of self-government. It was clear that any idea of independence in the foreseeable future was far from the minds of those in charge of the French Overseas Ministry in the summer of 1958.

My very frank conversations with African students and officials were particularly important to me because they provided background on the Franco-African political situation in France as well as in Africa. The students insisted upon the urgent need for all African territories to set up republics run by Africans. Unlike the students, most African officials seemed to be talking, at least during June and July, about independence to be achieved at some undetermined moment in the distant future.

It was my good fortune to interview Léopold Senghor in August, shortly after his return to Paris from the important July Congress of his political party (Parti du Regroupement Africain), held at Cotonou in Dahomey. Mr. Senghor was still somewhat disappointed that his proposal for a federal republic within a confederate union had not been fully accepted by the Congress. Senghor's proposal had provided the overseas territories with the possibility of achieving the status of states, which would have meant nominal independence; he insisted upon the inherent right to independence rather than upon immediate independence. The opposition, consisting of African youth groups, students, and labor union members, however, who opted for immediate independence, carried the day.

It became increasingly clear even to me, an outsider, that General de Gaulle and his Cabinet had already made the decision on the fate of the overseas territories. As early as the first week of August 1958 it was evident that France was to offer federation to the overseas territories with the stipulation that the choice would be between association or secession. Furthermore, the overseas territories would have to take a stand on the Constitution of the Fifth French Republic in its entirety, not just on those portions that concerned the territories alone. Thus the territories would face the option of remaining under French influence or being cut off—entirely or only in part— from French assistance.

As the summer wore on, I wondered increasingly about the Franco-African situation and the outcome of the September Constitutional Referendum. The Referendum would afford some of these French African territories the opportunity to seize their much-talked-about independence. Yet there seemed to be no indication that General de Gaulle was the least perturbed about this possibility. In fact, De Gaulle did not let the revolt of the French Army in Algeria or the struggle of the two major African political parties to change the Constitution keep him from setting out for Africa. He confidently took off for an August tour of the African continent while I was still in Paris. The French leader had made up his mind to travel 13,000 miles in order to convince forty million inhabitants of French African territories that they should accept the new constitution and membership in the new French community of free states. Apparently, General de Gaulle had convinced himself that for most Africans the advantages of an association with France far outweighed the attraction of independence.

I felt that this French leader was seeking to establish that by an act of free determination the peoples of Metropolitan France and the overseas territories would vote to accept membership in a community of free peoples. But I submit that De Gaulle never expected in August 1958 that his efforts to enlist the support of Africans would run into opposition in Guinea, a French West African territory.

I followed with great interest the reports on the reception tendered General de Gaulle as he made his way through Africa, in the hope of getting some indication of the sentiment for or against the September Referendum. The French newspapers reported that the General received a mixed reception as he traveled, ranging from sporadic applause to enthusiastic cheers. Upon reaching Guinea, General de Gaulle was greeted by some cheers as he rode from the airport to Conakry, but the welcome lacked warmth. In the Guinean Council Chamber came the confrontation of De Gaulle with the dynamic labor leader Sékou Touré, in the course of which the latter informed the French leader that the people of Guinea preferred "freedom in poverty to riches in servitude."

With the harsh words of the Guinean leader ringing in his ears, General de Gaulle reached the airport at Dakar in Senegal, only to be met by a crowd of jeering demonstrators demanding immediate independence and urging De Gaulle to "go home."

No official whom I met in Paris during De Gaulle's African tour felt that the incidents in Conakry and Dakar augured anything unusual as far as the September Referendum was concerned. The impression seemed to prevail that General de Gaulle had conveyed his desire for an affirmative vote to his African constituents and had thus ensured an overwhelming victory for the new Constitution of the Fifth Republic.

Indeed, General de Gaulle did achieve a victory, for on election day, September 28, 1958, all the French territories except one voted to accept the new constitution. Only the French West African territory of Guinea indicated its desire for immediate independence.

I had returned to North Carolina some three weeks before the Guineans went to the polls to cast their fateful No vote, but had kept in touch with the situation through the French newspaper *Le Monde* and correspondence with friends in Paris. But I would not have predicted before the election that Sékou Touré would have been able to get 96 per cent of the Guinean voters to go to the polls and reject General de Gaulle's appeal to become a part of the French community. At the time I was not aware that Sékou Touré had succeeded in getting his chief political rival, Diawadou Barry, to support the drive for a No vote, ensuring a unified stand among the Guinean people.

CONTENTS

FIRST AMERICAN
AMBASSADOR TO GUINEA

I
The Call

In the fall of 1958 my wife and I were living in Durham, North Carolina, where I was chairman of the Department of Modern Foreign Languages at North Carolina College. One morning in October we received a letter from a friend with whom I had taught in New Jersey thirteen years before. She was now retired and still living there. She wrote a pleasant letter, bringing us up to date and eventually asking, "Are you looking around for a new job?" I wasn't, and we were puzzled how such a rumor could have started, though they are by no means rare in academic circles.

This was only the first of a series of letter from friends who had been colleagues in New Jersey, Alabama, and Georgia. They had moved along to teaching positions in places as widely scattered as Wisconsin, New York, and California, but they all asked much the same question. We became even more curious about how such a story could have sprung up all across the country within a couple of months, and we wrote back asking what had given them the idea. The replies came that an investigator, apparently from some private organization, had called on them and asked all sorts of questions about my wife and me. What kind of people were we? What kind of parents? How did we stand in the community? Why had I left my previous position? But since no questions had been asked concerning our loyalty, our friends concluded that the investigator was a private one and not an FBI agent, and they assumed that the prospective position had nothing to do with the Government.

We were at a loss to explain to our friends what was happening. I had been investigated by the FBI in 1957, but that had concerned top-secret clearance in connection with my serving as a member of the Advisory Committee of the President's Committee on Government Security. I soon forgot about the queries as I turned my attention to the preparation of a paper on Jean-Paul Sartre and Existentialism scheduled for presentation at a meeting of language teachers in April 1959.

To be free to spend evenings at the library of Duke University, across town in Durham, I began eating dinner between 4:30 and 5:00 P.M. On April 1 I arrived home as usual at 4:00 and was greeted at the door by my wife, who said that a person-to-person call had come for me from Washington just ten minutes before. "Just as I was telling the operator you were not home yet but were expected by 4:30, I heard a woman's voice on the other end of the line say that the White House would put through another call at 5:30."

"This sounds to me like an April Fool joke and I don't intend to be caught by it," I said. "You and I both know that Fred [my brother, who was special aide to President Eisenhower] has never called us from the White House during the whole time he has been in Washington. When the phone rings next time, just ignore it."

"I think it would be wiser to answer it," my wife said, "because it might actually be an authentic call."

"Do whatever you think best."

At that moment my son came in to ask if I would help him warm up his pitching arm and bat a few flies and grounders. He reminded me about his Saturday ball game. I promised him faithfully to spend the following afternoon with him and his teammates.

After dinner I was on my way to get my briefcase when the phone began ringing; my wife hastened to pick up the receiver, then turned and beckoned to me. The operator asked my name and said that Mr. E. Frederic Morrow at the White House wished to speak to me. I heard a deep voice say "Hello." It certainly sounded like my brother.

"John," he continued, "I am somewhat pressed for time, but I wanted to let you know that the State Department would like you to come to Washington for an interview as soon as possible."

"The State Department?" I asked. "You know I don't know anybody in that outfit, and besides, don't you government employees have anything better to do than waste taxpayers' money on April Fool jokes?"

There was silence for a moment, and when my brother continued speaking, his tone made it clear that he didn't fully appreciate my reference to jokes and taxpayers' money.

"Just a moment, John. I give you my word that this call

is on the level. It's about some kind of assignment in Africa. Will you come up tomorrow?"

"I can't get up there tomorrow. Furthermore, I can't go charging off on some African safari right in the middle of the semester."

"At least," he continued, "you ought to come up to find out what the State Department has in mind for you."

"Tell them," I replied, "that I cannot come to Washington until the day after tomorrow."

"I'll expect you. Stop by my office and I'll see to it that you get over to State," he promised. "By the way, please tell Rowena it's a pity she has such a hardheaded husband. Tell John, Jr., to keep that pitching arm in shape and I'll catch a few this summer."

I reported my brother's closing remarks to my wife and son, and we started wondering about the kind of cultural program the State Department might try to develop in Africa. My son said he thought the United States Information Agency had more to do with U. S. cultural affairs abroad than the State Department. I said that this could be so, but it was true also that the Department had a Bureau of Educational and Cultural Affairs.

I set out for Washington the following evening by Pullman from Raleigh, but only after having spent a rigorous two hours batting ground balls and flies and giving some last-minute coaching to my son and his teammates. I wished them well in their upcoming league game, which, incidentally, they managed to win, 5-4.

I arrived at the Executive Office Building, now called the

White House Annex, a half-hour before my 9:30 appointment at the State Department. When the White House guard at the gate saw me getting out of the taxi he spoke up before I could ask how to reach my brother's office. "You have to be Mr. Morrow's brother. I might even have mistaken you for him, but I already waved him through here at 8:30." I waited at the gate until one of the staff secretaries came down to lead me through the security maze.

My brother introduced me to several of his colleagues, each of whom remarked about our close family resemblance. During the few moments of discussion with Fred, I discovered that he could throw no additional light on the reason for the interview. He asked me not to forget to call him after my conversation with Loy Henderson, Deputy Undersecretary of State for Administration, and then walked with me to the outside gate and a waiting taxi.

The closer I got to the State Department the more I questioned the wisdom of coming to Washington without knowing the purpose of the visit. I recalled the stories I had heard about the Ivy League atmosphere within the Department and the stuffiness and even snobbishness supposedly prevalent among career diplomats. I had occasionally seen Loy Henderson's name in the newspapers and knew that he was one of the better-known career ambassadors who had served with distinction abroad as well as within the Department. He had been sent out frequently in the past as a trouble shooter, but I thought he had retired from the Foreign Service. Apparently he had stayed on or had been recalled to serve in this new capacity.

Upon reaching the Department, I went to the office of Joseph Satterthwaite, the new Assistant Secretary of State for African Affairs. Satterthwaite, a tall, friendly, scholarly-looking career diplomat, took me immediately to Mr. Henderson's office.

Mr. Henderson stepped from behind his desk as we entered and, after shaking hands, motioned us toward the leather-covered furniture on the opposite side of the office. I noticed that his hair and moustache were graying, but his step was still athletic. He had a kind face and a genuinely pleasing smile. His sartorial effect was impressive and his manner businesslike. He asked me about the campus at North Carolina College, about my work and the trip from Durham and Raleigh. With these amenities out of the way, Mr. Henderson broached the reason for the interview.

"Mr. Morrow," he said, "we have asked you to come to the Department because it has been decided, after very careful consideration, that you are the person we would like to send as our Ambassador to the Republic of Guinea."

Mr. Henderson made this startling statement in the quiet, reassuring tone of a surgeon talking to a patient about to undergo a delicate, serious, emergency operation. He was studying me from head to foot and removed his glasses as he awaited my reply.

Recovering from the shock and implication of his remarks, I replied: "Let me assure you, Mr. Henderson, that I am definitely not ambassadorial material. In fact, by training and by preference, I am a college professor, and I hope to be one for quite a few years to come."

Messrs. Henderson and Satterthwaite smiled broadly at this response, and Mr. Henderson continued: "We know more about you than you do about yourself, Mr. Morrow. We have read everything you have ever written and we know about your life and career. It's true that there are a number of candidates who are anxious for this assignment. In your case, you have not sought this post; instead, we have sought you. Among other things, we have been impressed by your knowledge of African affairs and French politics, your friendly relations with many Africans, your academic record, and your fluency in French."

Mr. Henderson made several other observations and concluded the interview by remarking that Secretary Satterthwaite and his deputy, James Penfield, would want to talk with me at greater length.

While Mr. Henderson was talking, the answers to some puzzling questions flashed across my mind. Here at last was an explanation for those queries received from our friends last fall. Did this mean, however, that a private concern had been asked to check on me before I was seriously considered for an assignment about which I knew nothing? How else could this official say that more was known about me than I knew about myself? I could have understood it if this had been a loyalty or security check following my nomination to a post. Who had decided as early as the fall of 1958 that I was to be investigated as a possible candidate for the post in Guinea? Was it possible that I had also been under the surveillance of the French authorities during the summer of 1958 because of my conversations with Africans and Algerians

and because of the questions asked of French officials at the
Overseas Ministry and at the Quai d'Orsay? I did not feel
exactly flattered if I had been given such attention; but, I
thought grudgingly, these people at State are more thorough
about some things than they are reputed to be.

Mr. Henderson stood up, and I realized that the interview
was over. As I shook his hand, I thought of some questions
concerning procedures for picking prospective ambassadorial
nominees. I had often heard it said that they were usually
wealthy individuals who had made sizable contributions to
the party campaign funds and expected to be rewarded by
some suitable ambassadorship. This alleged practice certainly
did not apply to me, a poorly paid college professor.

I had a long talk with Secretaries Satterthwaite and Penfield
about the problems confronting the United States in Africa
and especially in Guinea. After lunching with Penfield at a
hotel some distance from the Department, I went to brief my
brother on the events of the morning. He was pleased at hearing that I was being considered for an ambassadorship and
told me sincerely that he felt that I was the man for this difficult assignment. The Washington grapevine, he observed jokingly, would search in vain for any evidence of nepotism, since
he had known nothing about this move. He supposed that my
abiding interest in French-African affairs, evidenced for more
than a decade, and my presence in France in the summer of
1958 might have played a big role in connecting my name
with the Guinean post.

He was surprised by my seeming lack of enthusiasm, and I
admitted that I was tired, somewhat numb from surprise, and

feeling rather skeptical. I told him I was probably going to wake up in Durham only to discover that the whole thing was one bad dream.

It was not until I was on the train returning to Durham that it dawned upon me that at no time during my conversations with the three officials had I said outright that I would like to go to Guinea. On the other hand, I had not said that I would not go if appointed, nor had I requested the officials to remove my name from consideration.

From the day I left Washington early in April until almost the end of May, I never heard another word from Washington. Had I been foolish enough to talk about my trip to Washington and the nature of the interview, I would have had no proof of having been approached concerning an ambassadorship.

Finally, late in the afternoon of May 28, my brother called to say that he had just been informed by the White House Press Secretary, James C. Hagerty, that the White House was about to release the information on my nomination by President Eisenhower to the post in Guinea. The release would indicate that the President had sent my name to the Senate Committee on Foreign Relations. My brother promised to let me know as soon as he could get word on the date of my appearance before the Committee. This telephone call concerning a news release brought me the realization that the April experience in Washington had been no illusory episode, but the prelude to a confrontation with contemporary reality.

II

Preparations for Departure

From the moment that the announcement of my nomination appeared in the press until the hour when my family and I left New York aboard the ship *United States* on July 16, 1959, our lives were turned topsy-turvy. Telephone calls, telegrams, and letters began coming in from all over the United States wishing me well in my forthcoming appearance before the Senate Committee on Foreign Relations, chaired by Senator William Fulbright of Arkansas. Some of the congratulatory letters came from points as distant as Japan, Korea, Mexico, Germany, and Africa; one of the first came from Governor Luther H. Hodges of North Carolina. Newspaper reporters from the local and state newspapers called for interviews, and radio and television stations wanted to arrange broadcasts, but I was unwilling to make any statements until my appointment had been confirmed by the United States Senate.

This decision was not pleasing to representatives of the news media, but my reluctance to be interviewed was understandable. The last two ambassadorial appointees to appear before the Senate Committee on Foreign Relations—Mrs.

Clare Booth Luce and Mr. Ogden Reid—had been subjected to strenuous and extensive questioning, and some of the proceedings had even been televised. The appointees had not always been in the most comfortable of positions on the answering end of the questions put by the members of the Committee. I had had occasion to wonder why any citizen would subject himself to such a situation, particularly when he was being called upon to perform a duty for his country. In addition, there was much talk about the Senators' discontent because some of the noncareer appointees lacked knowledge of the language and the historical, geographical, and political aspects of the country to which they were assigned. There was a general feeling that the next noncareer person to appear before this Committee—whoever he might be—would certainly be in for a hard time.

While I was trying to make out final examinations for my language classes and prepare the yearly report and budget for the following coming year, I was confronted with the task of answering the huge pile of congratulatory messages. There was also the question of the date of the hearing before the Senate Committee on Foreign Relations. At one point it was scheduled for June 10, but was postponed because of other matters on the agenda. I did not appear before the Committee until June 16, but a whole lifetime seemed to have elapsed before that memorable day.

My unavailability to the press did not stem the flow of newspaper articles, and each mail brought clippings from papers in New York, New Jersey, North Carolina, South Carolina, Georgia, Alabama, and Washington. Three articles struck me

because of their very different approaches. The first appeared
in the *Durham Morning Herald* (May 29, 1959) under the
following heading: "Morrow Seen as Fulbright Challenge."
The Washington correspondent of this newspaper, Walter
Pincus, said among other things:

> Fulbright has put the last two political ambassadorial ap-
> pointees on the hot spot with the result that Clare Booth Luce
> later resigned after some awkward publicity, and Ogden Reid
> received committee approval only after a long and arduous
> day of close questioning.
> Chairman Fulbright is known to have told the State Depart-
> ment there would be no more confirmation of purely political
> appointees. . . .
> The Morrow nomination puts it squarely to Fulbright to
> follow through with this threat—but on a Negro appointee,
> with all the resultant political implications for the Democratic
> Party.

Pincus indicated that, in his opinion, I would receive
Senate confirmation without difficulty; southern Senators, he
asserted, did not plan any concerted opposition.

The second article, bearing the title "Morrow's Qualifications for Guinea Post," appeared the next day in an editorial
in the same Durham newspaper. The editor wrote:

> Dr. John H. Morrow of North Carolina College is well pre-
> pared to be Ambassador to Guinea, the post to which President
> Eisenhower appointed him Thursday.
> For the past eight years he has carried on intensive research
> in the specialized field of French colonial administration.
> Guinea was a French colony from 1880 until it was granted
> independence last fall.

Dr. Morrow has carried on research abroad principally in Paris. He spent last summer there. Through the State Department and the American Embassy he was enabled to make contacts with officials in the colonial administrative offices and also with representatives and deputies from the African colonies. Thus he has been able to acquire both extensive theoretical knowledge and an intimate, practical, and working understanding of the French colonies and their people.

This intensive and extensive research has resulted in the completion of the manuscript of a book on French colonial administration. It gives every promise of becoming a significant contribution to a better understanding of the French colonies and their relationship to the mother country.

Dr. Morrow speaks French, the language of Guinea, fluently. In his teaching, he stresses the spoken language and insists that his students acquire facility in conversational French. His earlier interest, before becoming absorbed in his study of French colonialism, was French literature.

The appointment is a compliment not only to Dr. Morrow but also to North Carolina College. Those connected with the college and its friends must be gratified at this unusual recognition of the abilities and work of a member of the faculty.

The third article set forth a point of view that directly opposed the one expressed in the *Durham Morning Herald* editorial. The only similarity between it and the *Herald* article was that it too appeared on the editorial page. The editorial, bearing the title "Job for a Professional," appeared in the June 2 edition of the *Washington Post* and read:

> With no reflection upon Dr. Morrow, who is Chairman of the Department of Modern Foreign Languages at North Carolina College, we wish that a professional diplomat had been nominated for this particular task.

In the first place, there is an element of condescension in the selection of a Negro as the Ambassador to the new African Negro Republic. It smacks of a segregated assignment system under which Negroes have traditionally been given such posts as the Ambassadorship to Liberia and occasionally to Haiti. At the present time there is only one American Negro career diplomat serving as a chief of mission. This is, of course, in no way the fault of Dr. Morrow. But until such time as qualified Negroes are assigned more generally as mission chiefs, the posting of one to a Negro country is likely to seem patronizing and invite resentment.

In the second place, and more serious, Guinea is a spot for an expert. Recent news stories, among them a report by this newspaper's managing editor, Alfred Friendly, have related that the Communist bloc has made Guinea a focal point of its first major effort to penetrate Africa. To make Western help available in such a situation is a job of great delicacy requiring the utmost in skill and experience.

Perhaps Dr. Morrow can supply said skill, and everyone will wish him well. But there would be more ground for confidence if there were evidence that the administration regarded the Guinea assignment as a challenge to the best man available irrespective of race.

The words in the *Washington Post* kept running through my mind as I traveled by train from Durham to Washington on the evening of June 15 to reach the capital in time for the scheduled appearance before the Senate Committee on Foreign Relations at 10:30 the next morning. After a hurried breakfast I went to the Department of State to report to the Senate liaison officer who was to brief me on the Committee hearing. As I got out of the taxi at the diplomatic entrance, I noticed that it was 9:30. I also became aware that I was apprehensive for the first time since I had become involved in this affair. I suppose that the *Washington Post* editorial had not contributed to my composure.

At the Department of State I was introduced to two other appointees who were to appear before the Committee. After we had exchanged the usual greetings, the briefing officer outlined the order of the day. I was then taken aside and asked about what I would do if the question were raised about "second-class citizenship." I replied that anybody who was fool enough to ask me such a question should be prepared for me to tell him where to go. I went on to say that if an A.B. and a Phi Beta Kappa key from Rutgers, an M.A. and Ph.D. with honors from the University of Pennsylvania, and a *Certificat Avancé* from the Sorbonne constituted the mark of a second-class citizen, then the Senate Committee would very well have to live with it. My anger at this point completely dispelled the apprehension I had felt.

When I asked why this question was raised, I learned that an "interested" American citizen from the state of New York had written a letter to a very influential person in Washington who in turn had passed on the letter to Senator Fulbright, challenging me because of "second-class citizenship." Senator Fulbright had had the decency not to circulate the letter but to turn it over to the Department of State for an answer. I was then shown the very strong reply sent in response to this letter and felt quite reassured. No such question was raised by any Senator during the hearing; the next time I heard about "second-class citizenship" was after I reached Guinea.

When we entered the hearing room in the new Senate Building, it was already filled with spectators. Senator Fulbright, Committee chairman, arrived shortly thereafter, accompanied by Senator Frank J. Lausche (Dem., Ohio), Senator Mike J. Mansfield (Dem., Montana), Senator Theodore Francis Green (then Dem., Rhode Island). Two other Senators, members of the Committee, joined the group later, but for the life of me, I cannot remember who they were.

The two other appointees who were to appear before the Committee were William M. Rountree, a veteran Foreign Service officer of seventeen years' experience, just completing a three-year term as Assistant Secretary of State for Near Eastern and South Asian Affairs, who was scheduled to go as Ambassador to Pakistan; and Dempster McIntosh, onetime president of Philco International Corporation, Ambassador to Uruguay and to Venezuela, and the first manager of the Development Loan Fund (1957–1959), who was to be sent as Ambassador to Colombia.

Both Mr. Rountree and Mr. McIntosh had appeared before the Committee before, and I could not see how, with their broad experience, they would have any difficulty. Mr. McIntosh asked to appear first because he had to attend a budget hearing of the Development Loan Fund. He was asked a few routine questions and excused.

Instead of calling upon Mr. Rountree, Senator Fulbright gave permission to the Senators from the state of Washington to make an unscheduled presentation on behalf of a fair which their state wished to sponsor. As these Senators talked, the minutes ticked by and it began to seem as if the proceedings would have to be adjourned for the day before Rountree and I could be questioned. Fortunately, the Senators finished their exposition at 11:30, and Mr. Rountree was called. After a few questions he was excused. My name was called at 11:35, and I came forward; that walk—from the rear of the hearing chamber to the table in front of the dais on which were seated the Committee members—was one of the longest I had ever taken.

I was hardly seated at the table before Senator Fulbright asked me to tell the Committee something about my life and education. I believe that I made one of the briefest statements on record. Then Senator Fulbright asked me if it were not true that I had graduated with honors from Rutgers University and that I had participated in athletics while in college. I answered in the affirmative. The Committee chairman then turned to Senator Mansfield and inquired whether he had any questions. The Senator from Montana proceeded to the most unexpected question of the day. Instead of asking me something about foreign affairs or about my fitness for a diplomatic post, he asked me what the subject of my doctoral dissertation had been. The strangest thing happened at that moment: I could recall the subject of my master's thesis, but I could not remember the answer to the question asked. As Senator Mansfield smiled, the title came to me: "The Comic Element in À La Recherche du Temps Perdu." Senator Mansfield said he felt certain that anyone who could master that lengthy work of Proust was equipped to take on the diplomatic assignment in question; he expressed regret that I was not being sent to a larger mission.

At this point Senator Green, the oldest member of the Senate, wanted to know the name of the head of the Guinean

Government, the official language of the country, and whether
or not I could speak the language. Senator Lausche asked me
questions about my family and wanted to know how I had
become so interested in advanced studies.

A reporter from *Time* (June 29, 1959) described the conclusion of my appearance in the following fashion:

> Said Ohio's burly Frank Lausche, with a nod to Arkansan
> Bill Fulbright, committee chairman, and sworn enemy of non-
> career diplomats: "I'm sure you are the type of man that lies
> dear and close to the heart of what Senator Fulbright feels
> should be a good ambassador." Added Fulbright genially: "I
> think it will be a good experience for you."

I felt somewhat numb when the hearing was over because
I had been waiting for questions on U.S.-African policy and
French-Guinean relations, and these had not been asked. I
didn't have the feeling of having participated in a hearing
conducted by Senators, but rather of having had the opportunity of talking with fellow professors from neighboring
educational institutions. It was not until later, when I reached
the Department of State, that I recalled that Senator Fulbright
had been a Rhodes scholar, a lecturer in law, and later president of the University of Arkansas; Senator Green had once
been an instructor in Roman Law at Brown University; and
Senator Mansfield had been professor of history and political
science at Montana State University.

My nomination was confirmed unanimously by the Senate
on June 18, 1959, and four days later I was sworn in by Wiley

Buchanan, Chief of Protocol, in the presence of Secretary of State Christian Herter and other Department officials, Governor Luther B. Hodges of North Carolina, and the members of my family. The deep regret that I had concerning this ceremony was that my parents, who had sacrificed so much for my brothers and sister and for me, were not alive to share this proud moment.

From this point on until sailing time, our work was cut out for us. We had the medical examinations and the inoculations, and received diplomatic passports. My wife, daughter, and son had the task of closing up the house in North Carolina and deciding upon what was to be taken to Guinea and what placed in storage. I was faced with briefings, briefings, briefings, which were supposed to prepare me for the problems that I would have to face.

We had decided, immediately after my confirmation, to arrive in Guinea as a family group—a fact which impressed the Guineans very much, as we later learned. My daughter Jean had just received her master's degree from Fordham University's Graduate School of Social Work, and we thought the experience would be invaluable for her. It was indeed a graduation present, as I had to pay the passage both ways because my daughter was just turning twenty-one. My fourteen-year-old son John had finished his sophomore year in high school, and the Guinean experience would certainly be of incalculable value for him. As it worked out, my wife, daughter, and son became the most effective American ambassadors to Guinea.

For the next three weeks I was engaged daily in a series of

briefings involving not only the Department of State but all the governmental agencies that played any part in foreign affairs. This proved to be a somewhat grueling activity in the heat of Washington, despite the air-conditioned buildings. It was small wonder that foreign diplomats bemoaned the Washington summers. The climate, with its humidity, however, provided a foretaste of what was to come in Africa.

As the days passed, I began to experience some misgivings. Despite the briefings, and the conscientious reading of available documents, I was finding it difficult to ascertain the current United States policy in Africa in general, and in Guinea in particular. I began raising this question each morning with the Foreign Service officer responsible for drawing up my schedule of appointments, and he assured me that this matter of policy would certainly be covered before my departure. I learned that a mission of the International Co-operation Administration (now the Agency for International Development—AID) had made a survey of Guinean needs and was preparing a report. I did not see it. The embarrassed explanation was given that the Department of State had not yet had access to it, and there was no way of their knowing at that point what recommendations had been made about the extent of aid which the United States might offer to Guinea. I was told that the U.S. Government was interested in securing Guinea's consent to a plan for guaranteeing foreign investments, and in obtaining Guinea's support on the regulations pertaining to the "Law of the Sea."

I began to assess the situation as it appeared to me just a week before the sailing date of July 16. I was about to be sent forth on a tough mission without a full knowledge of the ground rules my country was going to be willing to honor. It had not been possible for me, up to this point, to get official authorization to discuss any specific kind or amount of aid that might help ensure the viability of the struggling nation to which I was being sent. My newness to diplomacy did not keep me from realizing that I ought to have a clear idea of what kind of commitment, if any, the United States intended to make toward the economic, political, and cultural development of this African republic that was being courted by the Communist bloc countries.

I realized that the Bureau of African Affairs had come into existence recently as a result of a law passed by the Eighty-fifth Congress and was not yet fully organized. The friendly and likeable Assistant Secretary of State for African Affairs, Joseph Satterthwaite, was just settling into his new post and was beset with many problems, not the least of which was the effort to help develop an effective U.S. policy in Africa. Prior to the development of the Bureau of African Affairs, United States relations with Africa had been the responsibility of a bureau that also handled Near Eastern, South Asian, and African Affairs. It had been impossible, under the old arrangement, to give Africa the attention it merited. Then suddenly, during the period when the new Bureau of African Affairs was attempting to find its way, the problem of Guinea developed, bringing with it the delicate question of French-Guinean relations.

My sympathy certainly was with Mr. Satterthwaite, as it was next to impossible to deal with Guinean matters in the Department of State without consulting with the division that handled French affairs—namely, the Bureau of European Affairs. I soon learned that the Bureau of European Affairs exerted tremendous influence over policy decisions in the Department, and I began to wonder just how much success the new African Bureau would have in vital questions involving French-Guinean matters. It is not in any derogatory sense that I point out that many of the Foreign Service officers in the upper echelons of the Bureau of European Affairs in 1959 and 1960—as well as a number of officials higher up in the Department of State itself—were genuine Francophiles who had enjoyed extended periods of duty in France.

Originally I had been very much surprised that my Government had seen fit to call me out of a classroom to take on a task as delicate and as important as the Guinean mission. But after three weeks in Washington, my surprise diminished as I became aware that there just were not many senior Foreign Service officers in 1959 who were knowledgeable in African affairs, fluent in French, and totally acceptable to a newly independent African nation. I remembered that series of prophetic lectures delivered by Chester Bowles at the University of California in March 1956, in which Bowles had stressed the need for more people in the U.S. State Department with a special knowledge of Africa. Bowles had called for the assignment to Africa of more able Foreign Service officers who had a background in African problems and were free of racial bias. Bowles had pointed out that American representatives needed to be more aware that they had broader responsibilities than that of merely maintaining daily contact with colonial governments. Referring to his visits to four American consulates in Africa during 1955, Bowles disclosed that only one of these consulates had ever had an African to dinner. Bowles was of the opinion that American foreign policy was not adapting itself to the growing anticolonial movement, and he emphasized the necessity of creating a new U.S. foreign policy that would take more account of the African continent.

It took only a short stay in Washington for me to become convinced that scant attention had been paid to such warnings and suggestions. The Senate Committee on Foreign Relations had decided as early as January of 1958, however, to undertake a thorough review of U.S. foreign policy not only in Africa, but also in the Far East, Near East, South Asia, Europe, Latin America, and Canada. By July of 1958 this Committee had voted to report to the Senate a resolution authorizing a complete study of U.S. foreign policy. The Executive Committee of the Senate Committee on Foreign Relations then met in January of 1959 to consider proposals and determine which organizations were to undertake the proposed studies. This Executive Committee decided to request the Program of African Studies of Northwestern University, then under the capable direction of Dr. Melville Herskovits, to prepare the report entitled "United States Foreign Policy in Africa," which was published by the U.S. Government Printing Office on October 23, 1959. However, the Senate Committee on Foreign Relations did not hold hearings on this report until March 16, 1960.

Unfortunately for those involved in Guinean affairs at that

26

time, this important report appeared too late to exert any helpful influence on the American effort in Guinea. The real impact of the report was not felt until the Kennedy administration took over in January 1961. Until the Kennedy administration made the distinct attempt to change the U.S. posture in Africa in general, and in Guinea in particular, it was to prove exceedingly difficult to refute the bold assertion of the Herskovits report that the United States had never had a "positive dynamic policy for Africa."

Halfway through the Washington briefings I learned that the U.S. chargé d'affaires in Guinea had indicated that he wanted to return to the Department. This unexpected request, following only five months of duty in Guinea, was not well received by State Department officials, who anticipated possible misinterpretations of his sudden departure just prior to my arrival. Officials in other agencies responsible for briefing me wasted no time in drawing their own conclusions. They sought to draw me out concerning this unusual development. I asserted that this officer's desire to leave Guinea had nothing to do with my assignment there. After all, he had been working under great pressure with an inexperienced and insufficient staff. He had probably found serving in Africa quite different from serving in the Far East. He was probably handicapped by Guinean displeasure at the United States' decision to send a chargé d'affaires rather than an ambassador. I concluded with the observation that little was to be gained by speculation over a perfectly legitimate request to be relieved of an assignment. This officer was still in Guinea when I arrived, and he was very helpful in briefing me; but the fact that he wanted to leave—and did leave shortly thereafter—certainly did not boost the morale of his colleagues left behind.

As I continued my talks with State Department officials and those in other governmental agencies, I began to sense that there was an unwritten policy on Africa which would make it extremely doubtful that the State Department would produce in the foreseeable future a blueprint for coping with the profound political, economic, and cultural changes taking place throughout Africa. The prevailing Washington sentiment on Africa seemed to be that the United States should proceed with "deliberate speed" in any effort to aid the burgeoning African states—particularly those states where European nations had long held major interests. Washington officials were hopeful that the ties, economic and otherwise, which formerly had bound African nations to the British or French, would be sustained in some fashion.

I could understand why Washington officials favored such a practical point of view, for our country could not hope to undertake alone all the economic and technical assistance required by Africa. But these officials were ignoring the fact that most Africans greatly feared continued dependence upon former colonial powers. Indeed, continued dependence was being called "neocolonialism" by Africans opposed to such support.

In Paris in the summer of 1958 I had learned that Africans were looking to the United States as the world power most likely to help them make economic, political, and social progress. African officials and students had followed with great interest our policies in Europe and Asia after the Second World War and had come to believe that the United States would not only have a sympathetic understanding of African ideals and aspirations but also would stand ready to help realize them. These Africans were placing their hope on the facts that the United States had come into existence through revolution and had sponsored the principle of self-determination to the farthest parts of the globe. They were unwilling, however, to face the question of whether or not the emerging African nations had the industrial development and the related experience to absorb millions and millions of dollars of economic and technical assistance such as had poured into Europe under the Marshall Plan. Obviously, the economic aspect did not concern them as much as the question of world powers exercising moral leadership.

As the time drew near for me to leave Washington on the first leg of my journey to Guinea, I learned that arrangements had been completed for the delivery to Guinea—at intervals yet to be determined—of a gift from the U.S. of 5,000 tons of rice and 3,000 tons of flour. This news encouraged me as evidence that America was interested in the welfare of the people of Guinea. I was to discover a short time later that on the day of the arrival in Conakry, Guinea, of the first shipment of American rice, 5,000 tons of rice donated by Communist China were already stored in Guinean warehouses.

It was disappointing to learn that the State Department was in a position to allot only three scholarships for Guinean students to come to American educational institutions. One official felt that such grants served only to make foreign students more dissatisfied with their own country and less willing to return home. For my part, I was thoroughly convinced of the importance of the cultural exchange program, and especially of any program that would bring Guinean students to America, where they could profit from our excellent educational facilities and from personal contact with Americans of all races. I felt that a way must be found to enable Guinean students to study in institutions other than those in Communist bloc countries. I tried repeatedly before leaving Washington to secure a larger number of grants, but did not succeed.

To those who persisted in asking me if I did not feel that I was being sent into a rather hopeless situation, particularly since the Communist bloc countries had a nine-month advantage, I replied with an unhesitating No. The Communist bloc countries had had nine months in which to make mistakes. My only hope was that the Guineans were becoming increasingly conscious that the Communists were not twelve feet tall.

The liaison officers at the State Department arranged for me to make a courtesy call on President Eisenhower before my departure from Washington. It was during this call that I learned that arrangements were under way for a state visit by President Touré to the United States in October of 1959. President Eisenhower assured me that the United States would go all out to make the visit a success. He made certain observations on the problems confronting the United States in Africa as well as in Guinea. He emphasized the interest which our country had in the new African republic and asked me to convey this to President Touré. He reminded me that I was to be his personal representative in the Republic of Guinea and that no visiting American, regardless of rank, would outrank me in that regard. The President said that he had received excellent reports about my appearances before the Senate Committee on Foreign Relations and before numerous officials in the various governmental agencies responsible for briefing me. The President appeared to be in good spirits and in excellent health as he talked in a relaxed fashion, seated at his desk with his back to Pennsylvania Avenue, where the traffic moved in a continuous flow. As I rose to leave, I realized that I would not see the President again until October. I was hoping that things in Guinea would have taken a turn for the better by that time.

I left Washington and returned to Durham to complete the inevitable last-minute packing. My family and I then drove to New York.

As we boarded the *United States* in New York on the morning of July 16 for the first part of our journey to Guinea, the only one who felt sad about our departure was my son John, Jr. He had had to leave behind his Irish setter, Kim. It was not until the very last moment that John had consented to turn Kim over to a professor at the University of North Carolina in Chapel Hill, the father of three children who wanted a dog badly.

I was not the happiest person in the world as I set out on this mission, because my Government had not yet decided

upon a firm policy as far as Guinea was concerned. I resolved
to overcome this handicap by maintaining a foot-in-the-door
position, while attempting to win the confidence and the respect of the President of the Republic of Guinea, his Government, and his people.

III

Beginning of a Mission

I looked out the window of the boat train from Le Havre as it entered the Gare St. Lazare in Paris on July 21, and to my surprise saw waiting on the platform two American Embassy officers, William Witman II and David Korn, and my youngest brother, U.S. Army Sergeant William Morrow, who was stationed in Frankfurt, West Germany. Witman and Korn had remembered our friendly relations during the summer of 1958 and asked for the assignment of meeting us and arranging for our onward passage as soon as they had learned that we were traveling to Guinea by way of Paris. My brother had heard over the Frankfurt radio that we were passing through Paris, and he had come in the hope of seeing us.

A series of briefings had been arranged by the American Embassy in Paris for the afternoon of July 21 and the morning of July 22. Our departure from Orly Airfield was scheduled for the evening of July 22 on an Air France plane going to Dakar, Senegal. My wife, daughter and son, and my brother were taken on a tour of Paris while I was engaged in the briefings.

Ambassador Amory Houghton and his wife had originally planned a luncheon in our honor for July 22, to which they intended to invite members of the French Foreign Office involved in African affairs. This idea was vetoed by the Department of State because the delicate situation between France and Guinea made it inadvisable for me to have any contact with French officials while I was en route to Guinea. Ambassador Houghton had to modify the plan for the lunch to include only Embassy officers, their wives, and the rector of the American Episcopal Church in Paris and his wife. The Department of State veto of the original plan made it impossible for me to reach any of my African or French friends, either within or outside official circles. Later events proved that these precautionary measures had been taken in vain, for Guinean Ambassador to the United States Telli Diallo later charged me with consulting with the French before presenting my letters of credence to the President of Guinea.

The Embassy had arranged for us to stay at the nearby Hôtel Crillon in the ambassadorial suite. Our brief sojourn in these expensive surroundings provided me with painful but instructive experience. My travel orders provided only for the passage of my family from New York to Conakry, Guinea. I was the only member of the family who could legally stop off in Paris for consultation with the Embassy officers. This meant that I had to pay for the three rooms in the ambassadorial suite occupied by my daughter, my son, and my brother, and I had also to pay the additional charge for double occupancy of the room my wife and I shared. This edifying bookkeeping operation helped me to understand why people who work for our Government are so well versed in all kinds of curious governmental regulations.

My wife and I had decided not to attempt to arrange for separate flights to Dakar. Therefore we took off from Orly Field as a family group on the evening of July 22, and thirteen hours later, at 4:30 in the morning, the Air France plane put us down at the airfield in Dakar. Because of Air France protocol, I was the first passenger to leave the plane. It was a relief to get outside; the ventilating system had stopped when the engines were turned off. A slight breeze drifting across the airfield made the outside temperature more bearable.

Despite the earliness of the hour, our plane was met by the American Consul General in Dakar, Donald Dumont, and several African journalists, one of whom was carrying a portable tape recorder. When Mr. Dumont stepped up to introduce himself, I told him that only a dedicated Foreign Service officer would get up at that ungodly hour. He grinned deprecatingly, but his presence made the hour wait for the plane to Guinea pass quickly and pleasantly.

Meanwhile, the reporter with the tape recorder was requesting an interview for broadcast over Radio Dakar. This was the first of many such interviews conducted in French which I would be called upon to make while in Africa. I expressed my pleasure at the opportunity for greeting the people of Africa and said that I was looking forward to the establishment of firm rapport and understanding between the United States and the Republic of Guinea. I was also happy to have had the privilege of meeting Léopold Sédar Senghor, one of the outstanding citizens of Senegal.

35

An hour later we were aboard a second Air France plane en route to Conakry. I began to wonder about the kind of reception we would receive in Guinea—not just the official greeting at the airport but the reception by the Government and the people of Guinea. There was no question that the nature of the relationship between the Republic of Guinea and the United States at that particular moment in history left much to be desired. Even though Guinea had achieved its independence in accordance with procedures set up by the French Government prior to the September 28, 1958, Constitutional Referendum, our Government had not seen fit to recognize the Government of Guinea until November of that year.

The United Kingdom had been the first Western power to recognize Guinea (October 1958), and its lead was followed closely by the Federal Republic of Germany. Guinean officials, very sensitive about the slowness on the part of Western powers to recognize the legitimacy of their Government, had let it be known that they felt that the Western powers had held back out of deference to France, their NATO ally.

Our country waited until February 1959 before it sent any diplomatic representative to Guinea and then only a chargé d'affaires, who had had several tours of duty in China, and a young staff member who recently had entered the Foreign Service.

I was only too conscious that the Government of Guinea had had their Ambassador to the United States accredited in April 1959 and that I was reaching Guinea on July 23.

I reviewed some of the events resulting from the Guinean No vote, sponsored by the powerful Guinean labor leader Sékou Touré. In prompt retaliation for this "bold and fateful" action which had kept Guinea from becoming a part of the new French Community, General de Gaulle had ordered the immediate withdrawal of all French technicians, teachers, and government functionaries. The French withdrawal had been accompanied by ever-mounting rumors of the removal from Guinea of small arms for the Security Force, judicial documents and files, furniture, office supplies, medical supplies, and the uniforms of the police force. Supplies that could not be put aboard ships were burned. Whatever the details of this withdrawal, the mere fact of occurrence had deeply wounded the newly born Guinean national pride. Nothing had happened in the ensuing months to bridge the gap between France and Guinea.

While the United Kingdom, the Federal Republic of Germany, France, and the United States delayed recognition of the Republic of Guinea and hesitated to offer economic and technical assistance, the Eastern European Communist bloc nations moved swiftly to capitalize on a situation that offered excellent possibilities for establishing a strategic bridgehead in West Africa. Russia recognized the Government of Guinea on October 5, 1958, and other Communist nations lost no time in following suit. Bulgaria, Czechoslovakia, and Russia hastened to open embassies in Conakry. East Germans moved in to establish a trade mission. These nations offered Guinea barter trade agreements that involved the exchange of consumer goods, machinery, and trucks for Guinean agricultural products. Czechoslovakia had been extremely helpful in supplying—supposedly unsolicited—a gift of small arms, light artillery, and armored cars.

The arrival of the arms in Guinea during April 1959, accompanied by a group of Czechoslovakian "technicians" headed by a high-ranking army officer, had aroused great concern in the West and had awakened rumors that the Republic of Guinea was fast becoming a Communist satellite. At this point President Sékou Touré of Guinea revealed that he had sent a request for small arms for security purposes through the Government of Liberia to the United States Government, but had never received a reply to his request. (President Touré reiterated this statement during his October 1959 visit to the United States. No formal denial of the Touré claim was made by United States officials.)

Thoughts of these and many other facts and events coursed through my mind during the hour and forty-five minutes of the flight from Dakar to Conakry. It had been raining, but as the plane came in over the ocean and arched downward through the clouds preparatory to landing at the airfield on the outskirts of Conakry, the rain stopped. The sun broke through and the sky took on that deep blue tint seen in tropical regions. The plane circled over the main section of the city, and from this vantage point we had our first glimpse of the beautiful, tropical capital of Guinea, surrounded almost completely by the Atlantic Ocean, fringed with palm trees and dotted with varicolored buildings, the most prominent being the high-rise Paternelle office building, the Hôtel de France, and the Présidence (equivalent to our White House in color and purpose).

From the windows of the plane it was possible to see a crowd gathered on the balcony and in front of the airport entrance. Assembled on the tarmac were a band, a detachment of troops, and a color guard with the flags of the United States and Guinea. The plane taxied over to the tarmac, where the landing platform was rolled into position. Waiting on the ground was a welcoming party led by the Guinean Chief of Protocol, the Guinean Secretary of State for Foreign Affairs, the chargé d'affaires of the American Embassy, the chargé d'affaires of the British Embassy, and three American Foreign Service officers attached to our Conakry staff. The band, trained by a French musician who had chosen to remain in Guinea, played our national anthem and the Guinean national anthem, while we stood at attention in the hot morning sun. As the notes of the "Star-Spangled Banner" wafted across that airfield in faraway Africa, I felt the same tight feeling in my throat and the tingling sensation up my spine which I experienced eighteen months later upon hearing our anthem and seeing the flag aboard a visiting American destroyer.

The French-speaking Chief of Protocol and Secretary of State informed me that they would accompany me as I reviewed the troops. We walked up and down the two rows of troops and received a smart salute from the officer in charge. I returned the salute and stepped forward to shake the hand of the officer in charge of the detachment and of the band leader. I thanked them both and complimented them upon the appearance of the troops and for the music of the band.

Later on I discovered that this simple gesture, quite unmilitary in nature, won for me friends among the Guinean Army.

At the conclusion of the ceremonies on the tarmac, we were escorted by the airport police to the upstairs waiting room of the airport, set aside for visiting officials. There we met other members of the Guinean Ministry of Foreign Affairs. Cold soft drinks were served, and I found them quite preferable, even at 7:45 in the morning, to hot coffee, for the temperature and the humidity were making themselves felt. We descended to waiting automobiles, and a motorcycle police escort lined up outside. The escort consisted of ten police officers dressed smartly in white uniforms and mounted on Czechoslovakian motorcycles. The first car, an old, open Cadillac, had been lent by the Guinean Government for the occasion and was decorated with an American and a Guinean flag. All the cars in the procession belonged to members of the Guinean Government, with the exception of an old Ford sedan lent to our Embassy in Conakry by the American Embassy in Dakar. That old Ford with all its frailties and deficiencies was to be my official car for a long time to come—a spectacle somewhat inconsistent with our American representation elsewhere in the world. (My own new Buick arrived a long time before the official car, a new Mercury, came on the scene, and helped the representation of the American cause. The only other vehicle at the disposal of the Embassy was a green jeep.) As for the old Cadillac in which the Guinean Secretary of State, Fodé Cissé, and I rode into Conakry, it was the same car in which President Touré and Premier Nkrumah had traveled about Guinea during their historic meeting of May 1959.

I had been very much surprised and favorably impressed by our reception at the airport, but I was not prepared for what took place during the eight-mile ride in an open car from the airport to the Hôtel de France in Conakry. We had barely moved onto the highway and started in the direction of Conakry when the Guineans lining the road began to cheer, wave their hands, and shout *"Amérique, merci!"* I decided that this was an allusion to the arrival of our first shipment of rice and flour. At intervals spectators, attracted possibly by the police sirens, rushed to the roadside to wave and shout words of welcome.

The procession entered the main streets of Conakry, thronged with shoppers, onlookers, shopkeepers, workers, and children, and the people began to applaud and to sing. Above the noise could be heard the greeting *"Ambassadeur des États-Unis, soyez le bienvenu!"* Truly, I felt a warm glow that morning and an empathy I never completely lost despite the crises that came later. I had not expected such a warm greeting, especially in the light of existing U.S.-Guinea relations. Secretary of State Fodé Cissé revealed that broadcasts in French, Soussou, and Malinké had merely announced that the U.S. Ambassador was scheduled to arrive that day, July 23, 1959. The people had not been organized for any formal welcome. The crowds that gathered when President Touré returned from Saniquelli, Liberia (July 1959), and Patrice Lumumba visited Guinea (August 1960), made me aware of the vast difference between a formal welcome and an informal one.

The kind of welcome we received in Guinea was carefully

noted and reported by diplomats of the West and of the East, for everything that was done by the United States and by any one of its representatives was observed closely with the view of detecting possible implications for future U.S.-Guinean relations. The outside world was informed of what had happened during our arrival through a release that was filed possibly by a representative of the French press who was still covering Guinea. I was more interested, however, in an editorial appearing in the August 14 edition of the *Washington Post,* especially since it was this newspaper which had sharply challenged my appointment because of my color and my lack of experience in diplomacy and in dealing with Communists. The *Washington Post* observed:

> Not long ago we had occasion to comment upon the selection of Dr. John Howard Morrow, a distinguished Negro educator, as American Ambassador to the new Republic of Guinea. We observed that there was an element of condescension in the appointment of a Negro to a Negro country, and expressed the wish that a professional diplomat had been sent to this sensitive post. So far as the reception of Dr. Morrow was concerned, our misgivings appear to have been misplaced. His background of international experience will help him to represent the United States adequately in a newly independent nation subject to many pulls.
>
> Nevertheless, the principle of assignment by merit rather than by race still needs attention. For this reason we are happy that a white diplomat Deputy Assistant Secretary of State, Elbert S. Mathews, has been confirmed as the new Ambassador to Liberia. For years the post in Monrovia has been regarded as a segregated sinecure for Negro politicians chosen not for their ability but for their color. . . .
>
> Let us hope that the appointment of Mr. Mathews points to

the evolution of a genuinely color-blind policy meaning, not merely incorporation of more qualified Negroes into the Foreign Service, but also assignment on the basis of qualifications regardless of race.

It struck me as ironic that a mere outward manifestation— an airport ceremony or a cheering populace—would cause a newspaper like the *Washington Post* to reassess my chance for success in Guinea, a crisis post. Surely the basic situation had not changed in the least, for I had yet to confront the problems of this African assignment. Reading the editorial, I hoped that at the close of my tour of duty some criteria less fugitive than this might be used to assess the success or the failure of any mission, mine included. Yet I did sense, on my first day in Guinea and afterward, that the people of Guinea saw in me the symbol of all that the United States—even with its problems of racial discrimination and segregation—meant to freedom-loving people everywhere: Liberty, Justice, Equality, Self-Determination, Help for the Mistreated and the Downtrodden. This, I had to tell myself, is what that American flag meant flying on the old Cadillac; this is what the representative of the United States—Negro or white— meant to the people of Guinea. Perhaps this was what the *Washington Post* meant when it printed its second assessment.

Three rooms had been reserved for us at the Hôtel de France, which looked out on the ocean. Except for its louver boards—a concession to life a few degrees above the equator— the Hôtel de France appeared to be a grand Parisian hotel transferred to a tropical city. The hotel was still under French management, and the prices matched those of any large hotel on the Right Bank in Paris. The food and service would later begin to reflect the difficulties brought on by the severance of economic ties between France and Guinea.

The chancery had inadequate facilities, but I accepted them because of the difficulty of securing adequate office space in Conakry. The question about the chancery in Conakry was later raised in an article in the *New Leader* (June 27, 1960), entitled "In Guinea We Have Faith." It was written by Dr. Norman Palmer, chairman of the International Relations Program at the University of Pennsylvania, after a twenty-five nation tour of Asia and Africa. Dr. Palmer reported:

> The American Embassy was located on the second floor of an eight-story building. When I asked why no American flag was displayed—I was acutely conscious of the hammer and sickle so prominent a few blocks away—I was given lame excuses: a proper supporting base for the flag had not been found; the Embassy was in temporary quarters; the only flag available had 48 stars, etc. No United States Information Service office had been opened, though I was told that an acting USIS officer had been assigned to Guinea. The International Cooperation Administration had done almost nothing except to send several people to make surveys. By the end of 1959 no further evidence of ICA interest had been manifest.

Toward the end of an inspection tour of Embassy property I was still in a hopeful mood, however, as we drove from Conakry to a suburb called Donka to visit the official residence for the first time.

After a drive of some twenty-five or thirty minutes the driver swerved suddenly off the main road and drove along a winding, narrow road, lined by trees and thickets that gave

one the impression literally of entering the brush. After a few
moments, I saw in the distance a structure built of cement,
similar in appearance to a California ranch house. It had
been white originally, but the rainy season had deprived it
of any luster it may once have had. The grounds surrounding
the villa—as it was called—were overgrown with weeds and
thickets that seemed an excellent breeding ground for snakes.
(Subsequent clearing of the grounds proved that the guess
about the presence of snakes—large ones—had been only too
correct.) A wizened Guinean with a machete in one hand
opened the gate, and the car proceeded up the drive, as yet
unpaved, to the entrance.

When I learned that the Guinean who had opened the gate
was the gardener as well as the guardian, I wondered how he
spent his time; for the only things growing were the weeds,
vines, and thickets that cluttered the place. I wondered too
what the American Embassy staff had been doing. For almost
six months they had known that an ambassador was coming
to Guinea. For more than two months the identity of the
American chosen had been known, and his expected date of
arrival certainly had not been a secret.

The residence was not ready for us, we were told, because
there was a dearth of capable carpenters, plumbers, electri-
cians, and painters in and around Conakry after the hasty departure of most of the French. But I succeeded in getting the
administrative staff of the Embassy to locate the necessary
workmen within a ten-day period, which led me to believe
that the same thing could have been done before my arrival.
The excuses of the officer who had been in charge of getting

the residence ready were not impressive; I had already seen the houses and grounds occupied by him and by the chargé d'affaires. They were in excellent condition—not to mention the outdoor swimming pool with fresh water that went with one of the houses.

My first look inside the villa was no more reassuring than my view of the grounds. The plaster was already showing through the paint in some places on the walls and the ceilings, even though this villa, constructed only a few months ago, had never been occupied. The floors of the dining room and the living room or salon were done in an attractive charcoal-gray tile with a white streak, ideally suited for heavy traffic in a country having six months of rain and six of dryness. The salon, like the dining room, received ventilation through louver boards, and its size could be increased by opening folding doors that led out to a good-sized veranda, also covered with tile. The room designated on the floor plans back in Washington as the "master bedroom" turned out to be an ordinary-sized bedroom with an adjoining shower. At the end of the hall were two small bedrooms separated by a bathroom. Midway down the hall there was a very small W.C., opposite which were large clothes closets that could be entered through sliding wall panels. Just off the entrance leading into the salon was a small room equipped with a commode and wash basin.

To reach the salon, when entering the villa through the doorway that looked out upon a circular driveway, it was necessary to walk down two steps. To enter the dining room from the salon it was necessary to walk up two steps.

46

On seeing the small kitchen that was set off from the salon, I found it difficult to visualize how we would handle the dinners and receptions we would have to give. That this kitchen did serve these very purposes once we moved in is a tribute to the ingenuity and resourcefulness of my devoted and tireless wife.

There were no rooms in the residence for visiting dignitaries, which meant that these guests would have to stay at the Hôtel de France in Conakry. It was not always easy to obtain hotel reservations because many of the rooms were reserved for diplomatic representatives from the various embassies. The plans for enlarging the official residence, discussed often during my stay in Guinea, were never acted upon.

Not all the furniture earmarked for the residence had arrived. Other pieces, designated originally to be kept in the warehouse until our arrival, had mysteriously found their way into the living rooms and kitchens of houses occupied by American personnel at the post. The furniture for the salon was piled in the middle of the floor. Beds had not been put together. The oven of the kitchen stove, which ran on butane gas—a very scarce commodity in Guinea—did not work. It was not until some weeks later when this stove burst into flames that we got a substitute stove from the warehouse. It had been set aside for nonexistent ICA personnel, but no matter how meticulously equipment is assigned in Washington, it has a way of showing up in use in unexpected spots, and we had done our share. For that matter, many, many months were to pass before the Embassy silverware, tablecloths, and napkins reached Conakry; the administrative section in Conakry had forgotten to put through the necessary requisitions before our arrival. Fortunately, my wife had had the foresight to bring along our silverware in the personal luggage, along with other necessities. Only thus was it possible to begin without embarrassing delay the luncheons, dinners, and receptions demanded by protocol.

As I surveyed the situation at the official residence during this first inspection, I was very glad to have come without my wife. She might have found the appearance of the grounds and the villa as well as the interior disarray extremely frustrating. I was able to get that portion of the grounds closest to the main gate cleared off before I took her and our daughter and son to see their new home. The cleaning up of the entrance improved the villa's general appearance so much that when my wife did see the residence and the grounds for the first time, she immediately sensed their possibilities. From the moment of our occupancy my wife toiled until she succeeded in bringing beauty to surroundings which had been drab and forlorn.

A redeeming feature of the location of the residence was that the ocean lay just off the expanse of land extending from the house down to a small stretch of sandy beach. Often the lapping of the ocean waves and the voices of Guinean fishermen returning with the day's catch were the only noises that broke the all-enveloping silence of approaching nightfall. The tepid ocean water—despite the alleged presence of sharks, as reported by local inhabitants—was the chief source of recreation and physical fitness for my family and me. The small beach area was shared later with our neighbors, Ambassador and Mrs. Herbert Schroeder, when they arrived from the Federal Republic of Germany (West Germany). It was visited occasionally by the Bulgarian Ambassador and his family, who lived nearby, as well as by the Soviet Ambassador, who drove out from Conakry for a swim.

The Guineans who had worked as butlers, cooks, chauffeurs, and house servants for the French were now working for Guinean Ministers or other government officials. Many had left Guinea to seek employment in Dakar, Freetown, or Abidjan. I had to interview a great many applicants, none of whom actually had the qualifications for the jobs, before I selected three of the more suitable ones. I left to my wife the responsibility of training them. For a chef, I selected a Fulah in his early forties who had once served as a dish washer and kitchen helper in Dakar. As his helper I chose an alert young Malinké who knew nothing about working in a kitchen, but did know how to iron shirts. For the third employee, responsible for keeping the residence clean, I hired a young Fulah who spoke and understood only his own dialect. We retained the guardian-gardener, who spoke no French and only a smattering of Malinké, and whose dialect was Kissi. We retained also the chauffeur who had driven for the Embassy before our arrival. He was an intelligent young Soussou who spoke fairly good French.

It was inspiring and reassuring to see the manner in which my wife and daughter trained these employees and developed them into a smoothly working team with an unmistakable *esprit de corps*. They learned to handle effectively luncheons, dinners, and receptions given for members of the Guinean

Government, the diplomatic corps, and for visiting United States Senators and other dignitaries. Little did our guests realize the hours spent in teaching a former dish washer how to prepare delicate hors d'oeuvres or to cook French and American dishes; or in instructing two nervous young Guineans, who had never before served meals, to set a table correctly and serve without spilling soup or wine on décolleté guests. The gardener's inability to speak French proved to be no obstacle to his learning to understand that my wife expected him to clear the grounds of all undergrowth, keep the lawns neat, and plant beds of flowers. Before our stay in Guinea was over, the gardener could understand some French and had also developed some skill in gardening. He became our most faithful and trusted employee and saw to it that no harm ever came to our persons or to the Embassy property.

The fact that my wife was an excellent cook was an inestimable asset, particularly since it was impossible to obtain trained servants in Guinea. At the outset she had to do all the cooking for the dinners and the preparation of the hors d'oeuvres for receptions in addition to being ready on time to act as hostess. At first she had to go into Conakry to do the marketing—usually done by one's chef and his helper, if one had a real chef who knew what he was doing. The task of marketing became increasingly difficult as French ships stopped bringing fresh produce and meats to Guinea, and the shelves in the stores were gradually depleted. Fortunately for us, my wife and daughter had made it a policy from the very start to shop on the "African market" as well as in the stores still run by the French. When the French disappeared from the stores and shops in Conakry and Guineans took over, my wife and daughter benefited from having patronized Guinean merchants.

At times I thought my wife possessed the skill of a prestidigitator when I tasted the dishes she miraculously created. With eggs, fish, shrimp, chickens, mutton, rabbits, lobsters, *couscous,* manioc, avocados, tomatoes, rice, spinach, mangoes, pineapples, bananas, almonds, red and green peppers, and a host of other mysterious ingredients, she could prepare a dinner for twelve or a reception for 150 or more. The acclaim won by her cuisine in Conakry and Donka was well merited. It was necessary to have luncheon or dinner guests at the residence on an average of two or three times a week—not to speak of breakfasts or teas for the ladies—and to have receptions every two or three weeks, and I am keenly aware that my wife served above and beyond the call of duty. In the heat and humidity of the Guinean coastal region she also had to accompany me on the remaining evenings to dinners, receptions, and other affairs given by Guinean officials or members of the diplomatic corps. Through it all, including the six months of rainy weather and the six months of dryness each year, she retained her aplomb, patience, and sunny disposition.

The considerate treatment and the training received by the Guineans employed at the residence—news of which promptly reached the rank and file of the populace of Conakry and Donka—the volunteer work of my daughter as a nurse's aide in the hospital in Donka and later as a teacher of English in the Girls' Lycée, and my son's coaching of his classmates in basketball and tennis at the Boys' Lycée accounted to some degree for the warmth of our reception not only in Conakry, but in other cities and villages of Guinea.

IV

Meeting Touré

It was understood that I would present my letters of credence to President Sékou Touré at the first propitious moment after his return to Conakry from a trip to Liberia. I was to become accredited a week after my arrival in Guinea, or just three days after the President's return. This promptness in receiving me stood in sharp contrast to the delay in allowing some diplomats, including the Chinese Communist Ambassador and the second British Ambassador, to present their credentials.

I had been at our chancery only two days when I had to make my first decision involving protocol. A telephone call on Friday afternoon, from the Secretary of State for Foreign Affairs Fodé Cissé, invited my family and me to travel with him to Kindia (some one hundred miles from Conakry) on Sunday to meet President Touré on his way back from Liberia. This most unusual invitation created a problem because I had not as yet presented my credentials and had no authority to travel around the country in an official capacity. I conveyed this as politely as I could to Secretary Cissé, but could sense from the tenor of his reply that he had not anticipated a negative response. I told him that my family and I would be delighted to make the trip. He agreed to call for us at the Hôtel de France on Sunday morning at 7:30.

The Embassy officer who had been serving as interim chargé d'affaires and was due to return shortly to the United States, was quite taken aback by my acceptance of the invitation. I assured him that this would probably not be the only time that protocol would be thrown out the window during my stay in Guinea—and it wasn't.

Even before we got up on Sunday morning, we could hear the rain beating against the glass panes in the doors that opened out on a balcony overlooking the ocean. There seemed little likelihood that the storm would let up. Secretary Cissé appeared promptly at 7:30 with a chauffeur-driven Peugeot. The two-and-one-half-hour journey to Kindia along the winding but fortunately paved road was made in a rainstorm. Although we did not express the thought aloud, my wife and I wondered how the reception for the returning President would be staged under such conditions.

Neither the storm nor the deeply flooded spots at intervals along the road served to slow down the young Guinean chauffeur, who drove at an excessively rapid rate. I felt somewhat more at ease after Secretary Cissé cautioned the driver, in a mixture of French and Soussou, against "breaking the necks" of his American passengers, not to speak of his own. The pace slackened slightly.

The rain stopped the moment we reached the outskirts of Kindia. It became necessary to move extremely slowly because the streets were thronged with Guineans in a festive mood.

The women and girls were dressed in multicolored materials with matching kerchiefs on their heads. The men and boys wore long robes called *boubous* with flowing sleeves, that were in some instances richly adorned. Some men wore cloth hats of different colors that resembled the hats worn by U.S. sailors; others wore the astrakhan hats which were fast becoming the distinguishing feature of government officials and members of the Parti Démocratique de Guinée. The crowds made it impossible to get any farther by car, so the car was parked not far from the railroad station.

We went to the station on foot, taking in the sights and sounds. The people were singing freedom songs in Soussou, Fulah, and Malinké. Some were dancing to music by an interesting assortment of instruments, including flutes, xylophones, stringed instruments, and African drums. Acrobats were performing before applauding onlookers, who urged them on to attempt the impossible.

Word was passed around that the train bringing the President and his party to Kindia was going to be late, apparently because the train was stopping at stations along the way where crowds had gathered. This train trip suggested the whistle-stop campaigns of American presidential candidates.

Guinean officials present at Kindia decided to serve lunch to the personnel of some of the embassies waiting for the presidential party. As my family and I took seats in the restaurant of the railroad station, I noticed that a group of five men moved over as a body and took the remaining seats at our table, passing by a table with available places.

The youngest member of the group, a ruddy, round-faced

youth of medium height, sat down next to me and said in French, "Have you been in Guinea very long?"

I thought that I recalled seeing him at the airport on the day of our arrival, but I replied, "We have been here only a few days and we feel at home already."

"How do you like this Guinean climate?" he continued.

"We are finding it quite livable. In fact, it's neither hotter nor more humid than Washington was in early July. How do you folks like this change from the snows of Moscow?"

"Oh, it's not too bad," he countered, "but a few at the Embassy are finding it a little troublesome. However, when I leave soon for Moscow, it's only because I am going back for an appendicitis operation. It will not be on account of the climate."

"I had much more foresight than you," I said, "for I saw to it that my appendix was removed last April in North Carolina so that I could travel lighter."

I became aware that this young official was the only one of his party at the table who was making any attempt to talk to me or the members of my family. I noticed also that he was being closely watched by a tall blond Russian whom I dubbed the political commissar of the group. The other members of the Soviet delegation were content to speak in Russian and concentrated on the food. I passed on the word to my family that our luncheon "guests" probably spoke English. As I recall, no Russian Embassy official ever spoke a word of English to me during my entire stay in Guinea. My daughter reported later, however, that Ambassador Daniel Solod spoke to her in English as she was boarding a boat for the Los Islands, several months after Solod's arrival in Guinea.

"Would you have any objection," I asked, "to pointing out some of the diplomatic personnel here in the restaurant?" I knew that the first Soviet Chief of Mission had returned to Moscow because of illness and had been replaced by a chargé d'affaires. I had heard also that the Bulgarian Ambassador had been absent from his post for a long time because of illness.

The Soviet Embassy officer pointed out individuals from the Bulgarian and Czechoslovakian Embassies, and from the East German trade commission. He then wanted to know if I had asked to be assigned to Guinea and how long I intended to stay there. I told him that I was in Guinea because I had been sent there by the State Department at the request of the President. I said that I would be in Guinea longer than he would, especially since he was returning to Moscow to lose a prized possession, his appendix. I concluded by telling him that I was sure that he was looking forward to a speedy return to the sunny shores of Guinea. He smiled somewhat wryly but did not attempt to answer. On several other occasions before his departure, this young man attempted to strike up conversations with me, and it was clear that he had been assigned to this task. He and I knew that he was wasting his time, for all he had to report were generalities about the Guinean climate, swimming in the ocean, and appendicitis operations.

Lunch had been over almost forty minutes when a Kindia

official came to announce that the train was due in a few moments. Our host, Secretary Cissé, reappeared and said that the Guinean notables wanted my family and me to be in the receiving line on the station platform. Soon two passenger coaches and an engine that had seen better days came into view. Ten months from this day, this antiquated equipment would be replaced by new coaches and a sleek-looking diesel engine from the Federal Republic of Germany. As the train came to a halt, a young man with strikingly chiseled features, wearing a long white *boubou,* a gray astrakhan hat, and white sandals, stepped off the second coach, followed by a number of Africans and three Europeans. I knew without being told that this was President Touré.

Secretary Cissé had seen to it that my family and I had places near the beginning of the receiving line, and he stood close by to introduce us to his President. As Touré approached, he could be heard addressing congratulations and thanks to the town officials and party members of Kindia for their well-planned welcome. The Guinean leader was possessed of great poise and dignity. Secretary Cissé made the introductions and said that he had brought us to Kindia as his guests. President Touré smiled broadly, gave us a very warm welcome, and expressed the hope that we would have a very enjoyable stay in Guinea. In reply, I expressed thanks for the warm welcome, and said that I was looking forward to the establishment of closer and friendlier ties between my country and his.

After meeting President Touré and some of the members of his Cabinet, I was introduced to the Czechoslovakian

Ambassador, the Bulgarian Ambassador, and the Liberian Ambassador. I discovered that the three Ambassadors, at the invitation of the Government of Guinea, had traveled to the Guinean-Liberian border to accompany President Touré on his return to Conakry. The third European in the party was a Frenchman, Jean Boyer, who served as President Touré's press secretary and idea man.

During the reception later in the day at the huge residence of the Commandant of the Region, we had the opportunity of meeting and talking with the charming and talented young wife of President Touré. I was introduced to Dr. Félix Moumié, leader of the dissident Cameroons political party (UPC), who divided his time between Cairo and Conakry. Dr. Moumié seemed to be on excellent terms with President and Mrs. Touré as well as with the various Guinean officials present.

With the approach of evening, the welcoming ceremonies were moved to the local stadium, equipped with electric lights for the occasion. We were fortunate enough to have seats on the speakers' platform from which to watch the three-and-one-half-hour program. The first hour and a half consisted of a series of presentations by dance groups and acrobats in front of the platform.

I got the impression that President Touré was not so much bored with the proceedings as that he was beginning to show the wear and tear of his visit to Liberia, the long return journey, and the activities of the day. When the young African leader got up to speak, however, he seemed to become a new person. His excellent speaking voice electrified the crowd that was jammed, standing, into every inch of the stadium. President Touré, speaking in Soussou, reviewed the accomplishments of the Republic of Guinea since its independence. Secretary of State Cissé gave me a running commentary in French as President Touré cited the number of schools, dispensaries, and roads constructed by the Guineans themselves. The President stressed the valuable contribution made by the voluntary labor of the people, known as *investissement humain*. He exhorted his rapt listeners to maintain the same spirit and vigilance which had brought Guinea its liberation, and he urged them to work diligently to free all Africa. He was interrupted frequently by thunderous applause and shouts of approval. The applause continued at the conclusion of the speech, and did not cease until Touré and his party left the platform ten minutes later.

During the infrequent lapses in conversation on our return trip to Conakry, I turned over in my mind what I had seen, heard, and experienced that day. I sensed that the Guineans, while genuinely proud of their leader, were drawn by his magnetic charm and crowd appeal. Touré, young, strong, articulate, the epitome of the self-made man, seemingly had much to offer his eager people. The question that persisted was whether or not this man, who had led his country to independence, would be able to exercise the kind of leadership necessary to preserve it in the face of serious economic and social problems. I had seen the much-talked-about Sékou Touré in action, and what I had seen had been indeed impressive.

On the third day after President Touré's return to Conakry

—July 30—I presented my credentials to him. The Chief of Protocol called for me at the Hôtel de France at 10:00 A.M. in the ubiquitous Cadillac, preceded by a police escort mounted on Czechoslovakian motorcycles. After informing my deputy that he was to ride in a second car, the Chief of Protocol telephoned the Présidence to announce our departure. The police escort and the two cars pulled away from the hotel and moved slowly down the broad boulevard leading to the Présidence. It had stopped raining shortly before we left the hotel, and the sun was shining brightly as it had on the day of my arrival in Guinea. As the cortege entered the gates to the Présidence, the colorfully dressed guards standing on both sides of the entrance stairs came smartly to attention, their drawn swords glistening in the sun. The Secretary of State, waiting at the entrance, greeted me and escorted me to the upstairs office of the President. He nodded to the guards stationed outside the office, and one of them stepped forward and ushered us inside.

President Touré, dressed in a European business suit, smiling affably, rose and came to meet us. After shaking hands he motioned us to seats across the room where a young Guinean radio reporter stood waiting with a portable tape recorder. It was then that I realized that the four of us were to be the only participants in the ceremony. The three Guineans neither spoke nor understood English, so French became the order of the day.

President Touré began by expressing the hope that better understanding would be established between the United States and Guinea. He recalled that the United States had not recognized his Government at the outset, and he expressed the deep disappointment he had experienced when the United States had not answered his urgent request for small arms for Guinean Security Forces. He cited some of the problems facing Guinea in its struggle for independence and stressed the point that his country intended to be friendly with all nations that wished to be friendly and recognized Guinean sovereignty.

I presented my letters of credence to President Touré and conveyed to him the cordial best wishes of President Eisenhower for his personal health and happiness and for the peace and prosperity of the Guinean people. I told him that President Eisenhower was looking forward with great pleasure to his official visit to the United States scheduled for October 1959, and that the American people had followed with great interest the development of the Guinean Republic since its independence. I expressed the hope that Guinea would continue along the road to peace and national well-being, and assured President Touré that I intended to do my utmost to promote relations between his country and mine based upon mutual respect and confidence.

An informal period followed the presentation of credentials, and President Touré ordered champagne for me and fruit juice for the others. Remembering the advice of Guinean Ambassador Telli Diallo, who had said that President Touré would appreciate some personal remarks after the formalities were over, I told President Touré how much my family and I had enjoyed our visit to Kindia and our opportunity of meeting and seeing him in action. I ventured to tell him that my own advanced age, forty-nine, made it possible for me to advise him—such a youthful President, thirty-eight —about taking good care of his health, and about conserving his strength so that Guinea would have the full benefit of his leadership during its formative years. The President and his Secretary of State laughed heartily at the reference to our age difference, and they seemed pleased at the advice. I learned some time later that President Touré had been impressed not only by the interest I had shown in his health, but also by the fact that I had brought my family to Guinea and that we had traveled up to Kindia to meet him upon his return from Liberia.

As I studied the face of this handsome African leader, whose finely chiseled, ebony-hued features were lighted up from time to time by a very engaging smile, I wondered how it had been possible for him to lead his people to independence virtually under the very noses of the French administrators. I decided that this labor leader must possess some unique qualities to have been able to accomplish such a feat.

It was well known that Touré's move to achieve immediate independence had won for him the admiration, respect, and even the awe of young people of North and sub-Saharan Africa. For these youths, Touré personified bold, fearless action in the face of overwhelming odds. There were those who opposed Touré's break with France and predicted his failure. Everybody agreed, however, that this young leader had grit and determination.

Touré's disdain for the difficult and his propensity to move into situations considered by others to be dangerous or impossible stemmed from the fact that he was a self-made man.

Since his youth he had met with situations in which failing meant dying either physically or politically. The almost total lack of formal education proved no handicap to such an ambitious young man, who used his native intelligence, leadership, and gift for speaking eloquent French as well as at least two Guinean dialects to move from the office of Secretary General of the Postal and Telecommunication Personnel Union (1945) to that of Mayor of Conakry in 1955, Guinean Deputy to the French National Assembly in 1956, Secretary General of the 700,000 member African trade union (*Union générale des travailleurs de l'Afrique noire*) in 1957, and President of the Republic of Guinea in 1958.

It was significant for the future of Guinea that Touré's political party—Parti Démocratique de Guinée (PDG)—wing of the African political party, the Rassemblement Démocratique Africain, of which Touré was a vice-president—had won an overwhelming victory in the local elections of 1957. This had been the first election in French Africa under universal suffrage, and many Guineans had voted for the first time in their lives. Touré, an astute, farseeing politician as well as a natural leader, had appealed particularly to the women of Guinea to exercise their franchise and play a more important role in the affairs of Guinea and of Africa. Touré pressed for the building of more dispensaries and championed the cause of improved education throughout Guinea. He urged the construction of additional schools. He talked about the redistribution of land and opposed openly the system of chieftains or village headmen.

It soon became apparent, even to Touré's strongest political opponent, Diawadou Barry (well-educated son of a Fulah chieftain and leader of the political party, the Bloc Africain de Guinée), that it was time to join forces with Touré. This decision on the part of Diawadou Barry meant that on the eve of the September 1958 Constitutional Referendum sponsored by the De Gaulle Government, Sékou Touré had already at his disposal, a smoothly functioning political machine.

Prior to the Constitutional Referendum, Touré's party alluded to his possible kinship with Samouray Touré, the Guinean warrior who had fought so fiercely against the efforts of the French to take over Guinea between 1891 and 1898. Samouray Touré had resisted the French until the very end, when he was betrayed, captured, and deported to Gabon, where he died in captivity in 1900. Sékou Touré's resistance against the French in 1958 was compared to that of Samouray Touré some sixty years earlier, and it provided a rallying point for Guineans during the crucial weeks that preceded the Referendum.

Throughout all Guinea, songs were composed and sung in the dialects Soussou, Malinké, and Fulah, pointing out the similarity between the exploits of Samouray Touré and Sékou Touré, and lauding the efforts of the latter to put the French out of Guinea forever. The songs compared Sékou Touré to the elephant, *Syli,* an animal of great strength and one most difficult to handle when aroused. These songs were heard day and night over the radio, in the city squares, and in the village streets.

Women as well as men traveled over the paved and un-

paved roads and into the brush to urge the Guinean populace to stand behind Sékou Touré and to go to the polls to
vote *Non*. The role of the women in stirring up feeling
against the French presence was extremely important. They
composed songs and created dances to incite their compa-
triots to rise up and oust the French. Touré would not have
been assured of victory had it not been for the women.

No American political campaign has been more successful
in reaching the voters than the campaign conducted by Touré's
political party prior to the Referendum vote. At the same
time that the Guinean No vote on September 28, 1958,
changed a former French West African territory into an independent republic, it placed the reins of leadership firmly in
the hands of Sékou Touré.

This was no mean feat in a nation that had been torn by
tribal rivalries and divided by many language barriers; where
more than 90 per cent of the people were considered illiterate,
and whose dwellings varied from the ultramodern brick
homes and villas of members of the Guinean Government to
the thatch-roofed clay huts of agricultural workers out in
the brush.

Empowered by full accreditation, I set out on my official
calls on the Guinean Ministers, and received as well as returned the visits of various members of the diplomatic corps.
Interestingly enough, the only member of the Guinean Government upon whom I did not call during this period was the
President of the National Assembly, the Honorable Saïfoulaye
Diallo, son of a former Fulah chieftain, and known as the

Number Two Man of Guinea. For some reason which was never explained, his office did not give the Guinean protocol officer a definite time and day for an official call. I had friendly conversations with Diallo at receptions and dinners at the Présidence, but I would never make that protocol visit.

No specific instructions had been given me before leaving Washington concerning protocol in respect to receiving or returning the visits of diplomats, but it was immediately obvious that visits were to be exchanged with all envoys who had mutual diplomatic representation in our respective capitals.

I received and returned, therefore, the visits of the Ambassadors of Bulgaria, Liberia, Czechoslovakia, the Israeli Republic, and the United Arab Republic. I also exchanged visits with the chargés d'affaires of the United Kingdom, the Federal Republic of Germany, Yugoslavia, France, Italy, and Switzerland. I decided to await the arrival of the new Soviet Ambassador and did not return the visit of the Soviet chargé d'affaires. The Nationalist Chinese representative, who was stationed in Monrovia, Liberia, made a trip down to Conakry to call upon me. I did not, of course, exchange visits with the Ambassadors of North Vietnam, Communist China, Cuba, and Outer Mongolia, nor did I have any social contact with these individuals at the various affairs sponsored by the Guinean Government. I did manage, however, to keep fairly well abreast of the diversified activities of this interesting foursome.

The members of the Guinean Government were quite sensitive about recognition and establishment of diplomatic relations on the ambassadorial level. They had not completely forgiven the United States for having delayed recognition, and for having followed initially the example of France in sending a chargé d'affaires to Conakry instead of an ambassador. Guinean officials did not object to the practice observed by Italy and Switzerland in having their envoys accredited to more than one country, for Guinea itself was following the same procedure. They were not happy, however, that the British Ambassador, accredited to Liberia and Guinea, lived in Monrovia and left Guinean affairs almost entirely in the hands of a chargé d'affaires in Conakry. The British chargé d'affaires, Hugh Jones, an exceptionally capable career officer, had established excellent relations with Guinean officials, but the latter still wanted a British representative of ambassadorial rank in Conakry. The British acceded to this wish a year or so later. The Federal Republic of Germany replaced their chargé by an ambassador several months after my arrival in Guinea. By the time of my departure from Guinea in March 1961, the following countries had ambassadors in Conakry: Bulgaria, Czechoslovakia, Cuba, Democratic Republic of Vietnam, Federal Republic of Germany, Hungary, Israeli Republic, Liberia, People's Republic of China, People's Republic of Mongolia, Poland, Switzerland, United Arab Republic, United Kingdom, United States, USSR, and Yugoslavia.

When the new French chargé d'affaires, Pierre Siraud, called at the chancery in Conakry in July, he invited me to a dinner he was giving the week following for a high-level commission coming to Guinea to discuss monetary problems between France and Guinea. This invitation placed me in a more difficult position than had the invitation to visit Kindia, extended upon my arrival by the Guinean Secretary of State. I thanked M. Siraud and promised to let him know the following day whether or not I would attend.

My acting deputy thought the dinner would give me the opportunity of meeting the visiting French officials. I reminded him that I had not as yet met the leading members of the Guinean Government. I told him that the French Commission was headed by the same official whom our American Ambassador to France had wanted me to meet in Paris, M. Roger Seydoux (later Ambassador to Morocco and head of the French delegation at the United Nations). But the State Department had vetoed my meeting the French in Paris. I felt strongly that the French Commission was not going to be able to solve the perplexing problems of the moment because of the very unfavorable climate in Guinea toward the De Gaulle Government. Furthermore, Guinean officials were already accusing Americans of never taking any action without first consulting the French. If the Guinean servants at Siraud's residence were to report that I had eaten and consulted with French officials before eating and consulting with Guinean officials, I would be placed in a most disadvantageous position before having established myself in Guinea. I decided, therefore, to send my regrets to M. Siraud.

Two days later I went to the French Embassy to make my return courtesy visit. When the old Ford, borrowed from our Embassy in Dakar, and bearing the American flag, came to a stop in front of the French Embassy, all the Guineans in the vicinity stopped to see who was getting out of the car. The

Embassy was on the same street as the Présidence and separated from it only by several short blocks. I knew that my visit would be known in the Présidence moments after I had entered the Embassy.

I was frank with the French chargé, telling him why I had felt it necessary to decline his first dinner invitation. As soon as I had established firm lines of communication with Guinean officials, I said, I would be more than happy to accept his hospitality. I realized fully that the situation between France and Guinea was made ever more difficult because of the personal feelings of the two leaders involved, and I assured Siraud that the United States would not interfere with French and Guinean efforts to work out a satisfactory settlement of their differences. My mission in Guinea, I concluded, was to establish friendship and understanding between the people of Guinea and my fellow Americans. I could succeed in this mission only by securing the respect and confidence of the Guineans.

My prophecy of the outcome of the negotiations between the French and the Guineans turned out to be correct. An impasse was reached after two days, and the French Commission left for Paris. This was to be the pattern followed by the negotiating groups who came to Guinea during my tour of duty.

It began to look at one point as if the agreements involving financial, cultural, and technical co-operation, signed by French and Guinean officials in Paris on January 7, 1959, might never be implemented. A major stumbling block was the question of the French Government's control over pension funds for Guinean soldiers retired from the French Army. The Guinean Government insisted that these funds should be under its jurisdiction and on deposit in Guinea. The French Government did not wish to relinquish its control—ostensibly to make sure that the Guinean veterans would continue to receive their pensions.

Another problem was Guinea's reported debt to the French Government. French authorities maintained that Guinea owed France repayment of the long-term loans arranged from FIDES (Fonds d'Investissement pour le Développement Économique et Social des Territoires). Guinean authorities held that Guinea should have access to the revenues collected through the years from the sale of Guinean agricultural and mineral products. They felt also that money earned by French teachers and technicians should not be returned to France, but should be spent—in part, at least—in Guinea.

My family and I enjoyed many dinners and receptions at the official residence of the French chargé after I had established rapport with Guinean officials. We reciprocated in kind during visits of distinguished Americans to Guinea. When M. Siraud became Protocol Chief of the De Gaulle Government, he was very helpful and hospitable to us during our later tour of duty in Paris.

By the time I got around to making my courtesy visit to the new Soviet Ambassador, Daniel Solod, his country had reportedly offered Guinea a $35 million line of credit. This offer had been made during the August 1959 visit to the Soviet Union of a Guinean delegation headed by National Assembly President Saïfoulaye Diallo and Minister of Public

Works Ismaël Touré, half-brother of the President. When I called on Ambassador Solod, I asked him if it were true that his country intended to give Guinea dollars to be spent as needed in other parts of the world. He laughed heartily and said that Russia had learned its lesson in China. The loan to Guinea was a true line of credit to be used for projects, equipment, and technicians.

The Soviet Ambassador, a former professor of mathematics, was reported to be the man who had introduced small arms into the Near East. He seemed to feel that I was making great headway with the Guineans. He gave the impression of being more outgoing than his predecessors, and he did have a sense of humor. He never admitted that he could either understand or speak English, and his French would have caused him some difficulty in gaining promotions had he been in the American Foreign Service.

V

At Work
in Guinea

The first formal request to come to the American Embassy
from the Guinean Government was made by President Touré
himself, when he asked our assistance in setting up instruc-
tion in the English language. The President told me about
the earnest interest on the part of all members of his Government to learn English. It had been necessary to use in-
terpreters in conversing with Prime Minister Nkrumah of
Ghana and President Tubman of Liberia. He indicated that
there was general agreement in Guinea that English should
be the second language of the Republic.

While the President was talking, my mind was busy with
all the things that could be done to grant this first Guinean
request. I assured President Touré that my country could
certainly help. He promised to co-operate in every way possible in any program that was established. I sent off an urgent
message to the Department, stressing the advisability of
promptly meeting this valid need.

Several weeks and many messages later, the answer to the
hurry-up request for an English language program came in

the person of Dr. Marie Gadsden, a very capable woman who did much toward developing good Guinean-American relations. She was assisted by two women secretaries from our Embassy, and by my daughter Jean. Dr. Gadsden and these three volunteers did much to convince the Guineans that the United States was interested in helping them make English their second language. However, the thing that bothered me was that in an emergency my country, with all its resources, sent out only one trained English teacher to a country of two and one-half million people. The Guineans were somewhat puzzled about this also, but they were too polite, in this particular instance, to ask questions about the apparent shortage of English teachers in America. It meant that Dr. Gadsden had to concentrate on teaching a few ministers and lycée teachers, while the volunteers taught English in the Lycée. The program was not augmented until many months later when a team of English-language specialists, headed by Dr. and Mrs. David Binder of Washington, arrived to spend a summer in Guinea. The English-language program reached its peak during the summer of 1960, and I regretted that this group had to leave Guinea at the end of the summer.

Shortly after my arrival, it became apparent that a morale problem existed among Embassy staff members. Some were none too happy about having been assigned to Africa. The idea still persisted that Africa was to a certain extent the Siberia of the American Foreign Service. (This idea, of course, was soon to be dispelled when the swift achievement of independence by African nations opened up new possibilities for rapid advancement to United States Foreign Service officers and offered the likelihood of becoming a deputy chief of mission or an ambassador at a much earlier age.) Some of the Americans were unhappy about a tour of duty in Guinea because they found it too difficult to adjust to Guineans, who were enjoying the fruits of their newly won independence.

Guineans, thrust into new positions of power, took their role as members of an independent government very seriously, and they stood ready to confront vigorously anybody who attempted to treat them in a manner even faintly resembling paternalism or condescension. They were puzzled by what they considered complacency and reluctance on the part of Americans.

The Americans were bewildered, and at times angered, by what they considered truculence on the part of the Guineans, who were often extremely sensitive, and always quick to insist upon their rights and upon just and equitable treatment at every step of the way. Certain members of the Embassy staff had the same misgivings about the ultimate fate of the Guinean experiment as had certain Washington officials. These misgivings made it hard for them to maintain open minds on the question of the best approach for America in this part of the world.

Diplomats from the West, and from the East initially, seemed to be quite oblivious to the importance placed by Guineans upon the dignity of the "African personality." This unfortunate oversight did not foster the improvement of relations. There was a failure to recognize the reasons why Guinean government workers, many of whom held positions for which they had not been trained, were overly sensitive and on the defensive about their inability to supply readily routine unclassified information frequently requested by friendly governments. A number of Western diplomats—including some U.S. Foreign Service officers—mistakenly interpreted the frequent Guinean harangues against imperialism and disregard for foreigners and protocol as conclusive proof of their unreadiness for self-government. They were unwilling to consider that these manifestations by the Guineans—such as the wearing of astrakhan hats by members of the Guinean Government—were designed to appeal to the masses, and possibly to divert attention from the difficulties created by breaking ties with France; that they were part of an effort to maintain independence.

When Guinean officials failed repeatedly to answer the many queries that came from various Foreign Offices, it often was not because they wished to be unco-operative or defiant, but was rather the result of their inability to secure authorization to release the information requested. The Guinean Ministers had to deal simultaneously with so many pressing problems that they had accumulated a backlog of unsettled matters. Some of the officials initially suspected that diplomats were spies placed in their country to ferret out and reveal to the outside world any inadequacies, deficiencies, or failures in the Guinean experiment. Those officials were extremely wary and uneasy about contacts with diplomatic representatives.

As for the reaction of the Foreign Service officers to my presence in Guinea, several thought the State Department lacked wisdom in sending to Guinea a man with no previous experience as a diplomat. It was not just that the assigning of a noncareer person meant that this was one more top position closed to career officers, who, understandably enough, considered an ambassadorial appointment the culmination of a successful career. It was perhaps the feeling of professionals that another professional should have been called upon to handle such a precarious situation. All these officers found themselves in the position, for the first time in their lives, of serving under a Negro. Several were bedeviled by the stereotypes so familiar on the home front concerning "second-class citizenship" and the possible lowering of standards. It did not take long to dispel their erroneous ideas. In the meantime, however, I did encounter from the staff some silent treatment, some slowness in complying with requests for vital information, some resistance to instructions that greater efforts be made to establish friendly contacts with their Guinean counterparts. There was a decided complacency among some of the Americans who were interested merely in maintaining contacts with other Western members of the diplomatic corps, of whom all but a few were equally ignorant about the thoughts and the objectives of members of the Guinean Government.

It is not possible to reveal here how I set about improving the morale and organizing an effective working organization at the American Embassy. However, by December of 1960 we had such a smoothly working team with such excellent morale that I was called aside by the Commander of destroyers from the U.S. South Atlantic Fleet, in port for an amity visit, and questioned as to how it had been possible to develop such *esprit de corps* in a hardship post.

Dr. Norman Palmer, mentioned above, who visited Conakry long before the Commander of the U.S. destroyers, had this to say concerning his impressions of my staff members and me:

> The First American Ambassador did not arrive until Summer of 1959; he was the chairman of the Department of French in a small Southern college and knew something of Africa. He has made a good impression, not so much because he is colored but because of his personality and his sincere interest in the country. But he is a complete parvenu in diplomacy, and he is operating in a country where a most astute and skilled professional is needed. In such circumstances, the State Department will normally assign a top-notch, experienced career Foreign Service Officer as Deputy Chief of Mission or head of the Political Section of the Embassy. The man who held both these posts did not possess such qualifications, although he is a fine and able officer with some African experience. He is a Class 3 Foreign Service Officer, and there were only two other FSO's in the Embassy, both very junior. The rest consisted of one Class 5 Foreign Service Reserve Officer and one Class 8 Foreign Service Staff Officer.

Dr. Palmer was rightly concerned with the staffing pattern of the Embassy; but had he made a return visit he would have noted that steps had been taken to strengthen the Embassy staff. He would have discovered also that our effectiveness and our posture had improved.

It should be evident that my task in Guinea was not merely a matter of vying with Communist bloc efforts to win the minds and the hearts of the people. It involved the attempt to win the respect and confidence of the members of the Guinean Government. It involved the effort to convince not only my own Government but the diplomatic representatives of other governments of the urgency of aiding the Republic of Guinea to achieve stability and viability. By no means the least of all, my task in Guinea included the challenge of winning the respect, confidence, and the loyalty of those Americans on the scene, as well as those who came later. I believe that I played a role in convincing Western diplomats and some American officials that our duty was to seek to understand the Guineans as they wore for the first time their newly won mantle of freedom. The Guineans stood ready to forego Western aid rather than lose their jealously guarded self-respect and dignity.

Behind the warmth of the greeting extended to my family and me upon our arrival in Guinea, and the genuine interest shown by President Touré and some members of his Cabinet, I could detect a good deal of anti-Western sentiment among high-ranking Guinean officials in general. It didn't take long to discover that these men were not at all convinced that the Western powers—especially the United States—intended to help Guinea and other developing African nations progress economically, politically, and culturally. Some of them suspected that the powers of the West were not so much interested in the welfare of Africans as they were concerned with the fate of their former colonial masters. I heard them hark back constantly to the failure on the part of the United States to honor their early, urgent request for small arms for security purposes and for radio communication equipment. They repeatedly challenged positions taken by the U.S. delegation at the United Nations on the question of Algerian independence, and expressed shock at the use by the French in Algeria of American arms under a NATO agreement. These officials wondered aloud about the existing military agreements between the United States and Morocco, and the United States and Libya. They appeared to be puzzled that the United States seemed so willing to pour millions of dollars in economic aid into Sukarno's Indonesia and so hesitant about doing the least thing for Touré's Guinea—after all, was not Sukarno Touré's very good friend (Sukarno visited Guinea in 1960)? Certain officials questioned me continually about racial discrimination and segregation in America, and about the treatment received by African and Asian diplomats assigned to Washington or the United Nations. Several said that they would never risk visiting the southern part of the United States.

I learned shortly after my arrival that the same question discussed by the *Washington Post* had been raised in Guinea, allegedly by Communist bloc diplomats—and one Western diplomat—concerning my "second-class citizenship." Stress had been placed upon the effrontery of the United States in sending to the Republic of Guinea a "black dupe of capitalism whose chief mission was that of deceiving naïve Guineans." When approached about this, I answered in about the same fashion that I had the first time the subject was raised in Washington, emphasizing the absurdity of having to waste time with such stereotypes. Moreover, the

Guinean Government acted promptly to dispose of all conjecture as to my status as the diplomatic representative of the United States. A statement appeared in the *Agence Guinéenne de Presse,* and word was passed by Guinean officials to members of the diplomatic corps. It was carefully pointed out that the Guinean Constitution ruled out all racism and considerations based upon color; the Guinean Government was interested only in the merit and worth of an individual, and in his willingness to respect the sovereignty of Guinea, as well as the dignity of the African personality.

It was disclosed that the Guinean Government had accepted readily and willingly the *agrément* presented on my behalf by the State Department, because it had requested specifically that an American educator rather than a career diplomat be sent. Guinean officials shared the belief that an educator might have more understanding and greater sympathy for the problems and aspirations of a developing nation. It was made known also that President Touré and his Ministers had been particularly impressed by my appointment because they had heard already from their Parisian friends about my sustained interest in the independence of African nations. Thus I came to know that the Guineans knew, as did the State Department, about my extensive conversations with African officials, students, and French officials during the summer of 1958.

It was not going to be possible to counteract the prevailing anti-Western sentiment by lecturing about the "virtues of democracy" or the "glories of free enterprise." The only way to gnaw away at this sentiment would be through persistent, pervasive, personal contact; through patient, intelligent, point-by-point answering of questions, assumptions, and charges; and through a sincere effort to seek mutual understanding and respect. In this personal-contact approach, initiated during my first dealings with President Touré and his colleagues, I was ably assisted by my family, and later by those dedicated members of the American Embassy staff who became convinced that this approach could improve the American image in Guinea.

I had read numerous conflicting stories in the press concerning the political coloration of President Touré, but I wished to reach my own conclusions. I listened carefully to his public statements and read those made before my arrival in Guinea. I had numerous frank conversations with him, and I traveled into the interior to talk with the Guinean people. I reached the conclusion that this fearless, tough-minded African leader was a fervent African nationalist, who had been quite impressed by Soviet and Chinese Communist claims of rapid economic development. I saw that he was intent on improving the African communal way of life by using those methods which could easily be adapted to that way of life. I believed that Touré was sincere when he formally rejected the principle of the struggle of classes in Africa, and that he was not going to welcome becoming a satellite of the Soviet Union. I decided that Touré believed that he could successfully apply democratic centralism to Guinean politics. I concluded that this African leader well understood that his Pan-African ambitions and his desire for recognition throughout Africa would be totally ruined if he allowed the East to dictate his policies.

I found it as difficult to convince Washington officials that Touré was an African nationalist, leading a country that merited help with its most serious problems of human suffering, as it was to convince Guinean officials that the policies of the United States supported self-determination of peoples, opposed racial discrimination and segregation, and favored help for developing nations of Africa and Asia.

My first confrontation with the Guinean Government concerning an American citizen came during the first part of August. This incident provided valuable insight into the inclination on the part of Guinean Ministers to do business only with the "head man" of an Embassy. They were influenced in this respect by their own experiences in running their Ministries.

Miss Joan Gillespie, a young American woman, arrived in Conakry to write articles on Africa for *The New York Times* and several American periodicals. Miss Gillespie had received her Ph.D. from the Fletcher School of Law and Diplomacy, had served two years as a Foreign Service officer, and had written a book on the Algerian liberation movement. She had been drawn to Guinea by the many conflicting reports on the Guinean experience in independence.

Miss Gillespie called on me at the chancery and let me know that she hoped to travel into the interior of Guinea to gather data for news articles. I told her that travel for civilians was still somewhat restricted and she would have to get permission from the Minister of the Interior, Fodéba Keita. The Embassy stood ready to help if possible, but the Guinean

Government had been most unhappy over some articles about their country which had appeared in American newspapers and periodicals.

Two days after Miss Gillespie's visit to the chancery, a call was received from the Ministry of the Interior. Minister Fodéba Keita wished to see me immediately. I sent word that the Minister could come right over. Another call came saying that the Minister would appreciate it if I would stop by to see him, as he was expecting several important phone calls that morning. When I arrived, I found Minister Keita, who was usually quite relaxed and jovial, pacing back and forth in his office. He reported that an American journalist had attempted to file a story reflecting seriously on the Guinean national honor. He had called me because he wanted me to ask this person to leave Guinea.

I asked the Minister what the journalist had said in the story, and he replied that she had been writing about a matter that concerned only Guinea and another African nation. The phone rang at that moment and a spirited conversation in Malinké ensued, after which the Minister turned and exclaimed that the woman journalist had just attempted to file a second story. He said that a Ghanaian in difficulty with Ghanaian authorities had been arrested at the airport in Conakry when he attempted to enter Guinea. The American reporter had witnessed the arrest. When she discovered that the Ghanaian was still in jail twenty-four hours later, with no charges against him, she began to question police officials. Not receiving an answer satisfactory to her, she sent off a dispatch to New York about the seizure at the airport. In her second wire she was questioning Guinean procedures for arrest and holding prisoners. She made comparisons between Guinean police methods and those employed behind the Iron Curtain.

I explained to the Minister the American concept of freedom of speech and freedom of the press, and said that his description of the journalist's activities suggested that she was performing the usual duties of her profession without in any way encroaching upon Guinean sovereignty. I told him that I could not ask the journalist to leave Guinea. In fact, one of my duties as Ambassador was to see to it that American citizens received full protection under the laws of the land.

Miss Gillespie was not asked to leave Guinea—either by the Guinean authorities or by me—but she was not given permission to go into the interior. After a week in Conakry she left for North Africa. All of us were greatly shocked when we learned some months later that seven weeks after her arrival in Tunisia, she had died following a brief illness.

In mid-August I was invited to accompany President Touré and his Cabinet on a trip to the bauxite-processing installations run by an international consortium known as FRIA, located some eighty miles from Conakry. This consortium was made up of investors from the United Kingdom, France, the Federal Republic of Germany, Switzerland, and the United States. An American corporation, the Olin Mathieson Company, was a large investor in the operation. I had already visited FRIA and had been taken on a tour of the huge installations by French officials of the Pechiney

Company that still ran the total operation of mining and processing bauxite for shipment to aluminum plants abroad.

When I arrived at the Présidence early on the Saturday morning of the trip to FRIA, I was surprised not to see the cars of my British, French, and German colleagues. I discovered that I was to be the only "foreigner." I was assigned to the car carrying Secretary of State Fodé Cissé and Minister of Justice Paul Faber, two excellent conversationalists. The time passed quickly despite the fact that a goodly portion of the trip had to be made over unpaved bumpy roads with sharp curves.

As we approached FRIA, we could hear the singing and applause of the inhabitants, who were lined up on both sides of the main road. Upon reaching the plant, we were taken on a guided tour and saw, among other things, a class in which several young Guineans were receiving rudimentary training in the use of mechanical and electrical equipment. It was hard to believe that just one year and a half earlier FRIA had been a wilderness of trees and thickets. All the heavy equipment and machinery involved in extracting and processing bauxite had been hauled either by rail on the spur track from the port in Conakry or by truck and trailer.

A reception given by FRIA officials and a buffet luncheon prepared by the Guinean women of FRIA followed the tour. I noticed at the reception that the Guineans from FRIA seemed to hover in one group and the FRIA officials in another. Although the Guinean Government officials and I mingled and talked with both groups, I could sense the tension. I discovered that there had been labor troubles at FRIA. Many

Guineans had been attracted to this area by jobs for unskilled laborers. Once the clearing had been done, the foundations dug, and the roads constructed, the laborers were no longer needed. Local Guineans were unhappy also because no Guineans were foremen or held the better-paying positions. The small apprenticeship training course had been set up on a long-range basis and did not help to meet the present demands for jobs.

Guinean officials had become increasingly conscious of the implications of the long-term operating agreement worked out for FRIA by the French authorities prior to independence. They contrasted their failure to see any "tangible" benefits from the FRIA operation with the situation in Liberia, where the Liberian Government was assured of at least 50 per cent of all profits from mining ventures in that country. Guinean officials could see no change in the management of FRIA; the French were as much in evidence in the running of operations as they had been in preindependence days. No Americans were employed in any capacity at FRIA. Guineans felt that some of the money earned by foreign personnel should be spent in Guinea and not sent abroad as savings.

After the luncheon President Touré made a speech in which he expressed the interest on the part of the Guinean Government in the continued functioning of FRIA. He stressed the necessity for the establishment of a closer understanding between the officials of the consortium and the Guinean Government. Touré traced the development of FRIA and asserted that it most certainly had a role to play in the future development of Guinea. His speech did not have any overtones that suggested that his Government might take over FRIA unless it were managed differently. This idea, however, was uppermost in the minds of French FRIA officials and accounted in part for their uneasiness. Apprehension seemed to prevail in some quarters that FRIA might be turned over to Eastern European countries.

President Touré, with his lively sense of humor, made the most of an incident that occurred during the luncheon. He told some of his Ministers in my presence that several of the ladies in charge of the luncheon had asked him the name of the tall, new Fulah member of his government. When he asked for a further description, he realized that the ladies were talking about me. The President and his Ministers were amused, not only because I had been mistaken for a member of the Government, but also for a member of a particular tribal group. I joined the laughter but could not help thinking that the Fulah tribe to which the Guinean ladies had assigned me was the one that had caused the French so much difficulty in the early stages of the colonialization of Guinea. This same group was becoming an increased source of concern for the Touré Government. Inhabiting Middle Guinea, also called the Fouta Djallon (from the Fouta Djallon Mountains, rising some 5,000 feet), the Fulahs represented more than one-third of the population of Guinea. These people, formerly organized along feudalistic lines, had become for the most part Muslims, and appeared to be more Hamitic than Negroid. Theirs was a difficult dialect, in which they took great pride. They were proud also of their cattle, counting their wealth by the number in their herds. The Fulahs still

88

showed great independence of spirit and loved to recall that they were descendants of the Fulani tribe that had conquered the area today known as Guinea, Senegal, and Mali.

Even before independence, Touré and his political party had taken vigorous action to displace the tribal chieftains and eliminate tribal differences. It had not been so easy to bring about co-operation among the tribes, even though this co-operation was apparent among the national leaders representing different tribal groups. The Soussou, concentrated in the coastal area of Lower Guinea, constituted another important tribe. The Soussou had been pushed out of the Niger valley by successive Fulani invasions. With the location of the capital in Conakry, the Soussou dialect had become increasingly important. The Malinké or Mandingo group, to which President Touré belonged, spread originally from Kankan in eastern Guinea to Bamako in Mali. This group came to settle around Faranah, the birthplace of President Touré, and Kankan, and spread down as far as Beyla. The Malinké were supposedly descendants of those people who had formed the great thirteenth-century Empire of Mali from which the present Republic of Mali derived its name.

There was one thing of which I was certain, however. I would not have wanted to be mistaken for a Fulah just prior to or immediately after independence, for a number of Fulahs did not support fully the severing of all ties with Metropolitan France. Most of the affirmative votes cast in the September 28, 1958, Constitutional Referendum had been cast in the Fouta Djallon region.

I did not find out until several days after this very pleasant trip to FRIA, on which I had been the guest of the Guinean Government, that it had provoked much discussion among members of the Guinean Political Bureau as well as among the Western and Eastern diplomats. The point of discussion was that the Guinean Government should not have singled out any one member of the diplomatic corps for a trip to an international consortium. The bloc members resented a gesture that seemed to represent recognition of a large American financial interest in Fria. Interestingly enough, the next invitation to the diplomatic corps to accompany President Touré and his Cabinet on a trip was not issued until April, 1960, when everybody was invited to travel almost four hundred miles by train from Conakry to Kankan to attend the national conference of the Parti Democratique de Guinée.

The case of mistaken identity which proved to be the most pleasing as well as amusing to President Touré and his Ministers was that which involved a member of the Guinean delegation to the United Nations and myself. Not long after my arrival in Guinea, Achkar Marof, number two man in the Guinean UN delegation (Marof later became Ambassador to the United Nations and developed into one of the most capable members of the Guinean diplomatic corps), returned to Guinea and made a trip into the interior, where he was mistaken for me. Marof is not as tall as I and has a moustache; but his features and color resemble mine. If our names were pronounced quickly with a French accent, they might sound somewhat alike.

At any rate, Marof had a hard time convincing Guineans in the interior that he was not the American Ambassador and that he was actually their representative to the United Nations. This incident was cited frequently by President Touré, who laughingly referred to Marof and me as perfect examples of the American-Guinean "exchange-of-persons" program.

VI

With Touré in America

As the time drew near for President Touré's state visit to the United States, I had to devote an ever-increasing amount of time to the many details to be settled before his arrival. The State Department readily assented to my suggestion that I arrive in Washington a week before the Guinean delegation to assist in last-minute preparations. I did not want anything to mar this visit, for I knew that all leaders in Africa were watching to see how Touré was received. They hoped to detect whether or not any changes in United States policies toward Africa were in the making. There was no question in my mind that Negro as well as white Americans were also going to be watching the drama inherent in the reception by one of the world's most powerful nations of the young African who had persuaded his people to say No to De Gaulle.

Before leaving for Washington I had tried without success to settle the question of transportation for the delegation from Conakry to New York. I was informed that President Touré wanted to be sure that the plane he boarded was not going to stop in any territory still under French jurisdiction. This ruled out using Air France. I could not get a satisfactory answer to the question about the regulations governing the use of Military Air Transport Service planes in the transportation of foreign heads of state outside the borders of the United States. No commercial airlines of Western powers, other than France, were interested at that time in establishing passenger service in Guinea. When I left Conakry for the United States on October 19, 1959, the only thing I knew for certain regarding the Touré visit was that Touré was going to keep his word and begin his series of state visits by coming first to the United States. He was not going to Russia first, as reported in some quarters.

It was not until after I had departed that the transportation dilemma was solved through the generosity of Prime Minister Kwame Nkrumah of Ghana, who placed at President Touré's disposal a Ghanaian Airlines plane to make connections with the Pan American flight. Thanks to Nkrumah, the delegation was able to board the plane that touched down late Sunday afternoon, October 25, at New York's International Airport. I did not have to be on hand in New York since the official visit did not start until the following day in Washington. President and Mrs. Touré and a party of six were met by Guinean Ambassador and Mrs. Telli Diallo, U.S. Protocol Chief Wiley T. Buchanan, Jr., and some New York officials.

The following day the Military Air Transport Service plane bearing the Guinean delegation landed promptly at 12:00 noon E.S.T., at the terminal in Washington. President Touré was the first to descend from the plane; he saw, among others waiting below to greet him, Vice-President and Mrs. Nixon, Secretary of State and Mrs. Christian Herter, Chief of Staff of the U.S. Army and Mrs. Lemnitzer, the dean of the diplomatic corps and Mrs. Sevilla-Sacasa, numerous Washington officials, and myself.

Ambassador Diallo, Vice-President Nixon, Protocol Chief Buchanan, and I accompanied President Touré to the speaker's platform and stood with him during the airport ceremonies. The twenty-one gun salute, the Guinean and American national anthems, and the inspection of the honor guard by President Touré were followed by brief speeches by the Vice-President and Touré. Nixon assured Touré America would receive him warmly because of the personal interest Americans had in him and the future of his country. Touré expressed the hope that his visit would bring closer relations between the United States and Guinea as well as with other emerging African nations. I was indeed moved by the occasion.

Our motorcade departure from the terminal en route to Blair House, the President's guest house on Pennsylvania Avenue, by way of the traditional Washington parade route, signaled the beginning of twelve of the fullest days I have ever spent. It was exhilarating to see the more than 250,000 people standing along the route to catch a glimpse of the man who had taken the dramatic and solitary stand against Charles de Gaulle. The Washington onlookers, I felt, were very generous with their applause, and the visitors were pleased with the warm reception on that chilly October day. The same was to be true in New York some ten days later, when an even larger crowd greeted the visitors during a ticker-tape parade from the Battery to City Hall. By mistake New York had on display Ghanaian flags instead of Guinean—they look quite similar.

The white-tie state dinner given that night by the President and Mrs. Eisenhower in honor of President and Mrs. Touré marked my second visit to the White House. As the car in which I was riding came to a stop under the portico, the real significance of the situation suddenly struck me, and I thought that only in America could something like this happen. I, a slave's grandson, was entering the official residence of the President of the United States. I was to be escorted down the long corridor to the East Room by an army officer in full-dress uniform. At the door of the East Room my name and title would be announced. Between the moment of leaving the car and mounting the White House steps, a feeling of deep regret swept over me; regret that my wife, daughter, and son were far away in Guinea and not on hand to share this historic evening with me; regret that my parents were not living to see the fulfillment of their prophecy that equality of opportunity would prevail one day in America.

When President and Mrs. Eisenhower and their guests had descended from the upstairs living quarters, those of us assembled in the East Room walked slowly as couples to the State Dining Room at the opposite end of the White House, where tables glistening with silverware, glassware, and emblazoned dishes, and decorated with beautiful flowers, awaited us.

I had the good fortune to be seated between the beautiful and charming Mrs. Gregor Piatigorsky, wife of the famous cellist, and Ambassador George V. Allen, then Director of USIA. The evening passed quickly and pleasantly. Polite speeches of welcome and acknowledgment were made by Presidents Eisenhower and Touré. Gregor Piatigorsky was in excellent form for the concert that concluded the evening. The real high point of the dinner, however, was the incredible performance of Colonel Walters, the interpreter, who presented us with the French version of Eisenhower's speech, and the English version of Touré's reply. Without notes or props, Walters gave the complete Eisenhower speech. He translated Touré's reply paragraph by paragraph, and this was no small feat because Touré spoke in long sentences. Only a skillful interpreter could have done justice to Touré's eloquent French. If Colonel Walters' virtuosity had impressed me at the dinner, I was even more impressed during the meeting that took place between Presidents Eisenhower and Touré the next morning.

A private meeting had been arranged for the two Presidents, but President Touré made it known that he wanted to be accompanied by President of the Guinean National Assembly Saïfoulaye Diallo, the Economy Minister, Louis-Lansana Béavogui, and Interior Minister Fodéba Keita. This change in plan caused me to accompany Secretary of State Herter and Assistant Secretary Satterthwaite to the Tuesday morning meeting at the White House. Guinean Ambassador Telli Diallo was also present.

We heard a very stimulating and exceedingly frank exchange of views between the two Presidents, with Colonel Walters again serving as interpreter. An hour later we left the White House to attend a meeting at the State Department presided over by Undersecretary of State Robert Murphy. A joint working party was set up after this meeting to iron out the details of a cultural agreement, which was signed on Wednesday morning by Secretary Herter and Minister Béavogui, who was appointed Acting Foreign Minister on the spot by President Touré for the signing ceremony. Ambassador Diallo and I were asked to sign as witnesses. (I later received an autographed photograph of the signing ceremony from Secretary Herter.)

President Touré made a memorable appearance before the National Press Club at the luncheon which immediately followed the Tuesday meeting at the State Department. He spoke and accepted questions from the floor which he parried with the skill acquired in debates at Paris, Dakar, and Conakry, impressing veterans of the press with his stage presence. That same night we attended a dinner at the Anderson House given by Secretary and Mrs. Herter—a most gracious host and hostess.

The afternoon of our last day in Washington (Wednesday, October 28), President and Mrs. Touré gave a luncheon in honor of President and Mrs. Eisenhower in the State Room of the Mayflower Hotel.

Between the official obligations of the Washington visit, President Touré, the Guinean delegation, and I journeyed by presidential helicopter to Mount Vernon; participated in a wreath-laying ceremony at the tomb of the Unknown

Soldier at the National Cemetery in Arlington; visited the AFL-CIO Headquarters for a talk with President George Meany; attended a reception at the Africa House given by the African Students Association; visited Howard University and met the president and faculty; and visited the Mosque of the Washington Islamic Center. President and Mrs. Touré attended a reception given in their honor by the Chiefs of Mission of Guinea, Liberia, Sudan, Morocco, Tunisia, Libya, Ethiopia, the United Arab Republic, and Ghana.

Contrary to the predictions of those who had dubbed Touré a "hard-headed Marxist theorist but not a Communist" and had insisted that he would straddle the fence between the East and the West to obtain aid from both sides, Touré made no requests for American aid during his visit. His failure to do so surprised even some career diplomats. The African statesman did not request aid at any one of the capitals visited during his forty-one day tour, and his return to Conakry in December contrasted sharply with the August 1959 return of National Assembly President Diallo and Minister of Public Works Ismaël Touré from Russia, bringing back the offer of a $35 million line of credit from the Soviet Union.

Touré later explained to his people why he had not requested any aid during his visit to America:

> We found in the United States a real desire to come to our assistance, but we refused to present demands of this nature. Everybody knows perfectly well the different needs of different people reported to be poor. It isn't radical nature which determines the quality of the needs, but the economic state.

Consequently, nations that really wish to aid Guinea or any other developing people don't have to wait to be solicited. We are certainly not going to disguise ourselves as beggars to explain our indigence which everybody knows, which everybody can appreciate, and to which each one can, loyally and in strict respect of our sovereignty, bring remedy. If we have placed African dignity so high, it is not to bargain it tomorrow against a few subsidies which, in the final analysis, could not radically suppress the effects of spoliation, exploitation, oppression, and depersonalization to which colonialism caused us to submit. (Secretary General, PDG, Rapport d'Orientation, April, 1960, p. 29.)

On the surface, the Washington phase of the visit had gone off with clocklike precision and had been eminently successful. Our guests, however, were quite disappointed on two scores, and rather dissatisfied on a third. They knew that President Eisenhower had come to the airport to welcome the President of Mexico and Premier Khrushchev of Russia. They had expected him to come to meet President Touré also. They were not impressed by the fact that Vice-President Nixon had cut short a Miami vacation to greet Touré, nor did they wish to accept the explanation that President Eisenhower's bronchitis kept him from attending the ceremony on that chilly autumn day. The Guineans were further dismayed when they learned that Protocol Chief Wiley Buchanan, who had accompanied Premier Khrushchev on his U.S. tour, had assigned his deputy to accompany President Touré. They assumed that their visit was being downgraded.

The third problem arose on the eve of Touré's departure from Washington and concerned the State Department interpreter assigned for Touré's speeches. The Guineans had been most happy with Colonel Walters. They were very unhappy when they learned that the interpreter assigned to cover Touré's speech at the Africa House would accompany the President throughout America. Their unhappiness was registered with the Department and with me in no uncertain terms, but it was not possible at that late date to supply a substitute. The situation became such before the tour was over that the Department had to provide another interpreter for the Touré speeches during the New York phase of the trip.

There had been so many invitations from groups and organizations wishing to entertain the Guinean President that the protocol division had experienced some difficulty in narrowing down the choices. There was also the question of the cities to be visited. New York, Los Angeles, and Chicago were selected without difficulty. Omal, Ohio, was added because Guinean bauxite was turned into aluminum at the huge Olin Mathieson plant there. President Touré wanted to visit Atlanta, the "gateway to the South," because his friend President Tubman of Liberia had visited this city during his 1954 visit to America. It was recalled that the Governor of Georgia had not received Tubman, and there was no desire on the part of American officials to risk a similar slight in the case of President Touré. The problem of a visit to a city in the South was settled when Governor Luther H. Hodges of North Carolina issued an invitation for President Touré and his party to be the guests of his state. This was a most fortunate turn of events, for it meant that the delegation went "down

South" with the assurance that they would be received with all the dignity and respect due foreign guests of the United States Government.

The State Department did not follow the usual procedure of having the American Ambassador participate only in the Washington and New York phases of a state visit, and sent me on the entire trip with the Guineans. I was delighted at the prospect of returning to North Carolina, where I had lived from 1956 to 1959. From the moment our plane landed at Raleigh-Durham Airport (Wednesday, October 28, 4:15 P.M.), where we were met by Governor and Mrs. Hodges and other officials, until we departed the next day (3:40 P.M.), the visit was an outstanding success. A large contingent of students and faculty members from North Carolina College and citizens from Durham had been at the airport to greet us. We were carried swiftly by automobile from the airport to the Carolina Inn in Chapel Hill. The Inn was operated by the University of North Carolina, and the visit of the Touré delegation marked the first time in its history that nonwhite guests remained overnight.

That night, on the campus of the University of North Carolina, a reception and dinner were given by Governor and Mrs. Hodges in honor of President and Mrs. Touré. Governor Hodges and President Touré made brief after-dinner speeches. The reception had been somewhat delayed by a news conference held by Touré with the more than thirty reporters covering the historic visit to Chapel Hill. The news conference afforded me a glimpse of another side of the Touré personality. Touré was repeatedly questioned about his opinions on the American race problem, discrimination, and segregation. Instead of seizing upon these questions as an excuse for getting off steam about America's Achilles' heel, the Guinean leader refused to be drawn into a discussion. He said that he could not answer such questions because he did not have the proper information.

Touré told the reporters that he was happy to visit the University of North Carolina and admired greatly the culture which it represented. He said that he had come to the United States with the hope of explaining and conveying a clearer understanding of Guinea's problems. To a question on Guinea's policy of neutralism in the cold war, Touré answered that he was concerned with the problems of developed and developing nations rather than with a struggle between the West and the East. He remarked that a poor man could not be asked to choose between diamonds and gold from New York, Paris, or Moscow, for he would take these things where he found them. Touré suggested that reporters should be more objective in reporting events in Guinea. He was alluding, of course, to the many articles by American journalists depicting his Government in a most unfavorable light. Touré concluded the news conference with the assertion that Africans already had the framework for a "United States of Africa," and needed only to define the content.

The next morning President Touré received an honorary degree from North Carolina College in Durham. He was luncheon guest of Dr. Hollis Eden, President of Duke University, also in Durham.

The *Durham Morning Herald* (Thursday, October 29,

1959) observed in an editorial entitled "Welcome Visit by New Nation's President":

> Durham gained an extra interest in United States relations with the new state of Guinea when Prof. John H. Morrow of North Carolina College became this country's first Ambassador to the former French colony.
>
> That interest is now heightened by the visit here of Guinea's first head of state, President Sékou Touré. As with all distinguished visitors, we are, of course, proud and happy that President Touré has included Durham and North Carolina in his personal inspection of the United States.
>
> The reason a leader of the nationalistic spirit sweeping across central Africa should include a Southern tour in his itinerary is obvious. While this reason requires that we not only shoulder the normal responsibilities of good hosts but take on the responsibility of showing how we are striving to overcome difficult problems, the chance to provide the Guinean President with a first-hand perspective on actual attitudes and conditions is a welcome one.
>
> President Touré, like us, has problems that should be better understood for his visit. Cut adrift by France with virtually no industry and a painful shortage of trained leaders in all fields, Guinea is truly beginning its national history from scratch.
>
> Dependency like the recently discarded colonialism is anathema to the surge of African nationalism which rightly seeks national integrity even if it seeks economic solvency. So President Touré looks on us, as he has said, "with the eyes of Africa," to find out if the United States "stands for freedom or foreign subjugation of peoples whose only demand is the application of the same principles upon which the United States was founded."

In a final interview with newsmen at the Raleigh-Durham Airport that afternoon, Touré said that he was very happy with his visit to North Carolina, and that he had received a good impression of the state and of its people. In reply to the query as to whether the visit had changed any of his conceptions of southern racial relations, Touré said that the visit had served to reinforce his previous conceptions. If his ideas had not been favorable before leaving Guinea, he would not have come. He had asked to see the South, Touré said, because he wished to see the diversity of the United States.

We were officially welcomed to Chicago the next day (Friday, October 30) by Mayor Richard J. Daley in an outdoor ceremony, followed by a luncheon given by the Mayor. We went to nearby Evanston to attend a tea given by Dr. Melville Herskovits, then Director of the African Program at Northwestern University. The Guineans enjoyed conversing with the lively and interesting Dr. Herskovits and his wife. We left Evanston to attend a buffet dinner given that night by Adlai E. Stevenson at his residence in Libertyville, Illinois. Governor Stevenson had resumed his law practice after his second unsuccessful attempt as a presidential candidate. In the very congenial atmosphere of the Stevenson home, Touré had the opportunity to meet some of the most influential men in American business.

Departing from Chicago's Midway Airport at 9:00 c.s.t. the next morning, we reached Los Angeles at 3:00 p.m. p.s.t. Saturday. It was during the flight to Los Angeles on the Military Air Transport Service plane that the members of the Guinean delegation really began to relax. They told me how much they had been touched by their reception by the American people. They were amazed at the vastness of Amer-

105

ica, the diversity of the people, and the freedom they enjoyed. They spoke respectfully of Eisenhower as a great military leader, and singled out Secretary of State Herter as the governmental head with whom they would like most to deal, because of his human kindness, honesty, sincerity, and respect for others. The Guineans stopped lowering their voices or changing the subject of conversation when I moved down the aisle or took an adjacent seat. We became a traveling team and remained thus until the trip was over. It was during this leg of the journey that President Touré dubbed Minister Béavogui, Minister Keita, and myself the "Three Musketeers" because we had stood together in all of the receiving lines and were the only members of the delegation who didn't drink fruit juice.

The calculated risk taken by the Department in assigning me to travel throughout the country with the group was paying off. The risk involved was the possibility of conflicts of personality among individuals traveling together in close quarters for a period of almost two weeks. The trip gave us the chance to get to know one another extremely well. The Guineans came to appreciate the United States more and to understand Americans better. The understanding which developed during this American visit withstood the crises and the strained relations that threatened United States-Guinea rapport during the rest of my tour of duty in Guinea.

The most significant event of the Los Angeles visit was the little-publicized meeting in Disneyland between President Touré and John F. Kennedy, who at that time was Senator from the State of Massachusetts. This private meeting had been planned originally for Sunday evening at the Ambassador Hotel, but had been changed to Sunday morning (November 1) at Disneyland. This was indeed a historic meeting between the two young leaders—one who was destined to become President of this great land, and one who had won independence for his nation. Senator Kennedy was then chairman of the subcommittee on Africa of the Senate Committee on Foreign Relations. He had expressed a point of view about Algerian independence that did not place him on the side of the French.

After introductions, the two men exchanged pleasantries about each other's youthful appearance and implied that youth was probably an important attribute for a leader in today's world. Senator Kennedy then expressed his keen interest in Guinean independence and in the struggle confronting Touré to maintain this independence. Turning to me, he said that, with all due respect to me and to the party which I represented, he would like to go on record as assuring President Touré that, if the Democratic Party came into power in the 1960 election, it would certainly have a great interest in the progress of Guinea and other emerging nations of Africa. Senator Kennedy wished President Touré well in his efforts to improve conditions in Guinea, and quipped that at least the latter had only one political party to deal with in Guinea, even though its symbol was an elephant (*Syli*).

In reply, President Touré expressed warmly his appreciation to the Senator for his willingness to confer with the delegation, and for his expression of interest in the Guinean experience. Touré assured him that such personal contact was most important in fostering better understanding and improved relations among nations. Touré made it clear that he and his colleagues had followed with great interest the Senator's stand on the question of Algerian independence. He concluded by wishing Kennedy continuing success in his future political endeavors. The next time they met was at the White House in 1962, when Touré conferred with Kennedy as President of the United States.

Something in the personality of this young, handsome, well-poised Senator struck a responsive chord in the Guineans. They were not more enthusiastic in their reactions to any other American than they were to Kennedy. They praised his youth, his courage, his astonishing knowledge of world affairs in general, and of the problems of developing countries in particular. They enjoyed the distinction drawn by Kennedy between the policies on Africa pursued by the two major American political parties. They believed what Kennedy had said concerning Guinea and Africa if the Democratic Party won the November 1960 election.

When the Guineans returned to Conakry, they were still talking about their meeting with Kennedy in Disneyland. There were no observers of the American political campaign of 1960 more interested than were the men who had visited America and had met Kennedy. Minister Fodéba Keita, after apologizing for appearing to interfere in the internal affairs of my country, told me that if he were an American, he would certainly vote for Kennedy because of the quality of his leadership. The Guineans were very happy when they learned in August 1960 that Kennedy, the Demo-

cratic presidential candidate, was sending Governor Averell
Harriman to Africa on a fact-finding mission that included
Guinea in its itinerary. They were even more elated when
Kennedy was elected President, and they were shocked and
genuinely grieved by the loss of the young President to an
assassin's bullet in November 1963.

After we left Los Angeles, we spent a night in Wheeling,
West Virginia, and the next morning visited the Olin Mathieson aluminum plant in Omal, Ohio. We reached New York
on Wednesday, November 4, where we were welcomed by a
ticker-tape parade, and President Touré was presented with
the key to the city by the Acting Mayor, Abraham Stark. This
ceremony was followed by a luncheon at the Commodore
Hotel given by Mr. Stark. Later that afternoon we met Governor Nelson Rockefeller at the New York Museum of Primitive
Art and were taken by the Governor on a personally conducted
tour of the Museum. Governor Rockefeller commented on the
collection in fluent French. President Touré inaugurated an
exhibit of Guinean art. A round-table discussion on Africa
with the members of the Council on Foreign Relations at the
Pratt House was followed by a dinner given at the Waldorf-
Astoria by the African-American Institute.

In the Waldorf lobby just before dinner Ambassador Diallo
disclosed that it had been decided to call off the state visit
to Canada, scheduled to begin Friday, November 6. Diallo
said that he could give me no details on the reason for this
decision, but that Canadian officials were being informed at
that very moment. I told Diallo that I hoped his delegation

had prepared a statement for the press, and he indicated that a statement was being prepared.

Ambassador Diallo and I entered the Jansen Suite where the dinner was to be held and found our places on the dais. We had hardly settled in our chairs before several reporters appeared on the floor below. One enterprising reporter jumped up on the dais, crawled under the table, and popped up next to my chair. He said the word was out that the Guinean delegation had suddenly canceled the visit to Canada, and wanted to know the reason. I told him I had no information, and I referred him to Ambassador Diallo. After conferring with the Ambassador, the reporter returned to me and repeated his question. I merely shrugged my shoulders. During the course of the evening the scene just described was repeated several times and gained a certain comic effect.

There were numerous conjectures in the press the following day about the cancellation of the Canada visit. It was noted that two Guinean Ministers had arrived the previous day, and questions were raised about reports emanating from Guinea of unrest and disorders among the people. Also suggested was the possibility of a serious disagreement between the Guinean Government and the corporation Aluminium of Canada, which extracted bauxite from the Los Islands just off the shore of Conakry.

Canadian authorities were very much put out at the unexpected turn of events because they had scheduled a full-scale program for the visit. The Guineans never did reveal the reason the Canadian visit was canceled.

On Thursday, November 5, President Touré attended a

luncheon in his honor at the United Nations, given by Secretary General Dag Hammarskjold. The Guinean President was to address a session of the General Assembly after the luncheon. He had been puzzled by the omission of my name from the list of those invited to the luncheon and had asked Ambassador Telli Diallo to inquire about this seeming oversight. Diallo was informed that it was customary for the United States to have only one Ambassador in attendance at such affairs, and since Ambassador Lodge had been invited, I was not. The Guineans felt that this was a very peculiar protocol arrangement, and expressed their regrets to me that I was not to be present.

I met President Touré and his colleagues after the luncheon and went with them to the General Assembly. The President's entrance was applauded by all the delegates with the exception of the French, who remained silent throughout Touré's speech. Touré declared in eloquent French that even though the newly independent African nations stood in need of assistance, they would not accept "paternalism" in any form, and they would not be taken in tow by either the Western or Eastern bloc. He said that Africa was seeking the kind of assistance that would help it free itself from foreign pressures and exploitation. He characterized the newly formed French Community of African states as a "union of rider and horse," and he asserted that the friendship of Africans was going to those who would help break the chains that imprisoned them. At the conclusion of his speech Touré was roundly applauded.

We were escorted to a downstairs conference room, where

the Guinean delegation met with the Afro-Asian group. I had not been told about this meeting and inadvertently went along with President Touré and his colleagues. The room seemed to be somewhat crowded, and I saw Krishna Menon of India conferring with several delegates. I asked one of the delegates standing nearby what was going to happen. He said that President Touré would address a special session of the Afro-Asian group. As I turned to make my way to the door, Krishna Menon called the meeting to order. The Guinean Ministers told me that I should not leave before the President spoke, so there I was.

At the close of the session, photographers took pictures of the assemblage. The Guineans were much amused later when they saw a picture in the newspapers with the caption "President Touré and his Cabinet," because I could be seen in the background. They thought it was amusing that their "American brother," as they now called me, had attended the Afro-Asian meeting by mistake and had been taken for a member of Sékou Touré's Cabinet.

Although the state visit ended officially with Touré's appearance at the United Nations, the State Department asked me to remain with the delegation until it left New York for London on Monday night, November 9. The decision not to go to Canada necessitated this shift in plans. The security officers remained on duty also. We were present, therefore, to witness an event which almost marred the good results achieved during the official phase of the Touré visit.

A certain New York impresario had convinced somebody that President Touré should come to Harlem for a parade and

ne 22, 1959. John Morrow takes the oath of office, administered by Chief of
otocol Wiley T. Buchanan and witnessed by Secretary of State Christian E.
rter.

The family at the swearing-in ceremonies. Daughter Jean Rowena, the Ambassador, son John Howard, Jr., Mrs. Morrow, and Secretary Herter.

The Ambassador, arriving at the *Presidence* in Conakry to present his credentials, is greeted by Secretary of State Fodé Cissé, and is received in the office of President Sékou Touré. *Information Guinée*

Accompanied by a Guinean newspaper reporter, Ambassador Morrow makes his first radio speech to the people of Guinea. *Information Guinée*

The Ambassador's residence at Donka, near Conakry, some time after the Morrows moved in.

October 26. Guinean Ambassador to the U.S. Telli Diallo (second from left), Vice-President Richard M. Nixon, and Ambassador Morrow stand at attention to greet President Touré and his party on their arrival at Dulles Airport for a state visit to the United States. *USIS Photo*

Units of the U.S. Armed Forces escort the Touré party to the White House. *USIS Photo*

President Touré is received by President Dwight D. Eisenhower at the White House. The U.S. President, suffering from a cold, had been unable to attend the Airport reception. *USIS Photo*

October 27. Concluding their second day in Washington, President and Mrs. Touré attend a state dinner given by the Secretary of State and Mrs. Herter. *USIS Photo*

October 28. Escorted by Major General C. K. Gailey, President Touré places a wreath at the tomb of the Unknown Soldier. *USIS Photo*

A cultural agreement between the United States and Guinea is signed by Sectary Herter and President Touré. Ambassador Morrow and Louis Lansar Beavogui, Guinean Minister of Economics, take part in the ceremony. *US Photo*

October 30. President Touré visits Adlai E. Stevenson at his Libertyville, Illinois, home. Two days later at Disneyland, Touré meets and confers with the then Senator John F. Kennedy. Ambassador Morrow accompanied the Touré party on the entire tour. *USIS Photos*

Back in the East, President and Mrs. Touré attend a dinner given in their honor by the Governor of North Carolina and Mrs. Luther H. Hodges at the University of North Carolina in Chapel Hill. *USIS Photo*

Winding up his tour in New York City, President Touré and Governor Nelson Rockefeller of New York visit the Museum of Primitive Art, where they admire a late nineteenth century woodcarving of the Nimba Ozbaga tribe of Guinea. *USIS Photo*

December 15. Back in Guinea, the first official guest is Senator Stuart Symington, who is greeted with the usual airport ceremonies. Secretary General Diallo, Senator Symington, Ambassador Morrow, and Secretary Cissé receive a salute from the Guinean Army's guard of honor. *Information Guinée*

September 30, 1960. Ambassador Morrow and Guinean Minister of Plan N'Famara Keita exchanged copies of the bilateral agreement for technical and economic assistance to Guinea, which they have just signed. *Information Guinée*

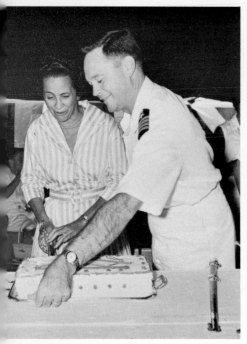

December. The U.S. Destroyer *Vogelgesang* called at Conakry. *Left,* at a party on board, Mrs. Morrow cuts the cake with the sword of Captain R. P. Foreman. *Right,* the Ambassador, going ashore, receives naval honors.

February 1961. To celebrate the return of Guinean troops from the Congo, the U.S. cruiser *Hermitage* paid a visit to Conakry. Rear Admiral Alan Reed entertains members of the Guinean government on board.

Ambassador Morrow on the Congo River with Robinson McIlvaine, then Consul
General in the Republic of Congo, who became Ambassador to Guinea in 1966.

The United States Embassy in Conakry. Arrangements were made for purchasing and renovating the building before Ambassador Morrow left Guinea. He received this picture as a birthday card in Paris in February 1962. It bore the message, "Happy Birthday, Mr. Ambassador, from your friends in Guinea," and was signed by the seven members of the Embassy staff.

a program at the 369th Artillery Armory. Many of Harlem's leading citizens knew nothing about these plans until they had been agreed upon. On a rainy Saturday afternoon Touré rode through the Harlem streets in an open car and stopped off at the Armory where a crowd had gathered to hear him speak.

As the President of the New York Chapter of the NAACP moved up to the microphone, a series of loud boos and whistles came from the audience. The Guinean Ministers and Ambassador Telli Diallo rushed over to me on the speaker's platform to find out what was happening and particularly whether this disrespect was directed toward their leader. They suggested that we leave at once. I was as puzzled as they, but I consulted hurriedly with New York officials, who informed me that a feud existed between nationalist groups and the NAACP. They assured me that no disrespect was intended for President Touré. The Guineans, though not completely reassured by this information, decided to stay.

Order was finally restored, but the NAACP official never did get the chance to make his welcoming speech. Touré's speech, delivered through an interpreter who had replaced the one so severely criticized by Ambassador Diallo, was well received. President Touré later brushed aside the incident and said that people all over the world had disagreements, regardless of color. One Harlem newspaper, the *Amsterdam News,* warned that such incidents might cause the State Department to make Harlem off limits to visiting diplomats.

A side effect of the Guinean visit to America became ap-

parent seven months later at a May Day celebration in Conakry. Until that time I had had no reason to recall an incident occurring the day we reached Los Angeles that previous
October. Ministers Fodéba Keita and Louis-Lansana Béavogui
had been very much impressed by the eye-catching maneuvers
and skillful riding of the motorcycle police escort during our
swift journey from Los Angeles International Airport to the
Ambassador Hotel. No sooner had we reached the hotel than
the two Ministers asked me to introduce them to the escort
squadron leader. With me as interpreter, they proceeded to
ask the policeman all sorts of technical questions concerning
the motorcycles. Pressed for time, I tactfully suggested to the
Ministers that we could get additional information later. The
matter didn't come up again, and I gave it no further thought.

On the morning of May 1, 1960, in downtown Conakry, I
took the seat reserved for me in the reviewing stand and talked
quietly with British chargé Hugh Jones and Israeli Ambassador Shlomo Hillel as we awaited President Touré and other
dignitaries. After a short wait the President appeared, descended from his new black Cadillac, and mounted the stand
amid the applause of the throng packed behind the police lines
along the broad boulevard. I was slightly puzzled at the con-
spicuous absence of the usual police escort, but forgot about
this as the ceremonies began. Suddenly, from the distance
could be heard a noise that resembled the sound of airplane
engines warming up. The crowd in the street turned as one
person in the direction of the sound, but those of us in the
stand could see nothing. At the precise moment when President Touré took his seat in the stand, there appeared a detail of

114

motorcycle police elegantly dressed in new uniforms and white gloves, and mounted on huge and powerful Harley Davidson motorcycles that glistened in the sun. The crowded boulevard resounded with shouts and the gleeful clapping of hands. From all sides of the square came the cry: *"Amérique! Amérique! Amérique!"*

I became conscious that the spectators crowded near the reviewing stand were looking in my direction and applauding. I did the only polite thing I could think of, which was to return the recognition by waving to them. How was I to let them know that I was as surprised as they were to see those motorcycles? No agreement had been signed between the United States and Guinea at that stage. These motorcycles must have been purchased as a result of initiative taken by the Guinean Government, with its own funds. The populace interpreted the miraculous appearance of impressive-looking motorcycles as further evidence of American interest in Guinean development. They might have been shocked to discover that I preferred assistance in the areas of health and education as evidences of American interest.

Seated just two places to my left in the reviewing stand that morning was Ambassador Vladimir Knap of Czechoslovakia. His usually smiling countenance was an interesting study in crimson and somberness. Looking at the Ambassador caused me to realize that on this day we had something in common—surprise. Knap was just as dumfounded as I to discover that those choice motorcycles so nobly supplied by his country through barter trade agreements had been replaced by American motorcycles. For him this meant a loss of face and an apparent closeness in ties between America and Guinea which he had had no cause to suspect until this sleight of hand on a May Day morning.

Of course, Knap was wrong in surmising that the new machines had any political significance; but I did enjoy the spot he was in. My colleagues in the diplomatic corps would have adjudged me the biggest hypocrite in Guinea had I tried to convince them that I was not a part of this plot to show off American technological superiority. I found out that the machines had been received in Guinea and hidden in a warehouse. Arrangements had been made for police officers to learn to handle the powerful motorcycles in secret in an outlying village. The machines were brought into Conakry for the first time that morning and unveiled just before parade time.

After the President's speech and the parade, I walked up to Ministers Keita and Béavogui, who were smiling broadly as I approached. I shook their hands and admitted that they had really put one over on me. What I did not tell them was that they had put one over on Ambassador Knap also, and had at the same time helped my situation in Guinea a great deal.

VII

Guinea's Struggle for Survival

President Touré in his first selection of ministers and ambassadors saw fit to place several of his closest friends, and also his half-brother, in key positions. This was as much a form of insurance as it was a matter of trying to make the best use of the talents of these faithful colleagues, some of whom had returned to Guinea from abroad at Touré's request. Touré was farsighted enough to see that in the days that lay ahead he would need to have around him men whom he could trust when the going got rough. His naming of his half-brother Ismaël Touré Minister of Public Works and Transportation did not cause the same reaction in Guinea as, for example, the late President John F. Kennedy's naming of his brother Robert Attorney General. In Guinea nobody talked about nepotism or saw anything amiss in President Touré's having a relative in his Cabinet.

There were non-Guineans who were forever conjecturing about differences between President Touré and Ismaël Touré and looking for a possible break in relations between them.

117

This was nothing but wishful thinking, because if President Touré had really feared his half-brother, he would not have allowed him to be the first to head a Guinean delegation to the United Nations. Furthermore, he would not have continued to send him on numerous very important and delicate foreign missions. Ismaël Touré was reputed to be very much impressed with the progress of the Soviet Union, but I recall his frank appraisal of road-building equipment and his decision that America made the best on the world market. The younger Touré was as intelligent as the President, and could be as charming when he so desired, but he was more distant and standoffish than most of the other Guinean Ministers. As was true of others, he had to go on so many missions abroad that his Ministry suffered from his absence.

President Touré appointed the congenial and likeable Louis-Lansana Béavogui, a former medical student, to the post of Minister for Economic Affairs, and later made him Minister of Foreign Affairs. Touré called back to Guinea his good friend Fodéba Keita, former head of the widely traveled Ballets Africains, and appointed him Minister of the Interior. Keita was shifted later to the post of Minister of National Defense and Security and thus placed in charge of the army and the gendarmerie. In the light of the military coups staged during 1965 and 1966 in several French-speaking African republics, as well as in Nigeria, it has become apparent that President Touré was attempting to make sure as early as 1960 that he could depend upon the forces bearing arms. The first Minister of Defense was N'Famara Keita, former Mayor of Kindia, and a very likeable person, one of the Guineans whose word was his bond. A natural leader, he was capable and ambitious. He later became Minister of Commerce and then Minister of Plan. Interestingly enough, he was replaced as Defense Minister by the sophisticated Fodéba Keita, reputed to be a man of means in his own right; he was also a man upon whose loyalty President Touré had reason to believe he could fully depend.

Telli Diallo, Guinea's first Ambassador to the United States and later head of the Guinean delegation to the United Nations (at present he is Secretary General of the Organization of African States, with headquarters at Addis Ababa), returned to Guinea at the request of President Touré. A brilliant lawyer who had served in French West Africa as a magistrate, Telli Diallo was one of the best-educated and best-trained members of the Guinean team. Although a personal friend of President Touré, he was not a member of the inner circle. For one thing, he did not hold membership in the National Political Bureau and stood little chance of ever being elected to this powerful body. Moreover, he had received much of his education outside Guinea and had lived and worked abroad. He was regarded as an intellectual.

I always felt that in some fashion Telli Diallo was trying to compensate for his superior training and trying to prove that he could be as extreme in his views at the United Nations or at Africa House in Addis Ababa as the most extreme member of the Guinean Labor Union. He always seemed out of character when he attempted to express in harsh terms the prevailing mood or line of his Government. He faced the ever-present possibility of being recalled, and there was no comparable post available for him with the Government in Guinea.

Naby Youla, Guinea's first Ambassador to France, to Bonn, and to London, had lived in France for many years and was reputed to be in business in Paris. He experienced little difficulty in making the transition from businessman to ambassador in the familiar surroundings of Paris, where he was known and considered quite capable. At the close of his tour of duty in Paris, Naby Youla was named Ambassador to Moscow. Youla refused to accept this assignment and was called home to work in the Ministry of Foreign Affairs. I understand that he has since been considered for another diplomatic post. Here at least was one Guinean who did *not* want to go to Moscow.

All these men, chosen to represent their country in various capacities, had one thing in common—the earnest desire to work without stint to ensure the success of the Guinean experiment. I respected them for what they were trying to do against great odds, even though I did not always agree with the tactics employed. A number of ministers had studied at the William Ponty school in Dakar. Telli Diallo was one of the few who went to France for further study. It was not easy for Guineans to go to France to study during the colonial regime because the Guinean quota for study abroad was infinitesimally small. Fodéba Keita, for example, got to Paris on his own initiative. There was no scholarship available for an advanced teaching degree the year he became eligible. Ismaël Touré did not get the scholarship which he hoped would open the way to study engineering in Paris, and had

120

to work on the Metro to support himself there. I sensed among these young Guineans the feeling that the French had failed to make available adequate educational opportunities, and had made it impossible for them to receive experience in high-level administrative positions. Guinea did not have cadres of civil service employees ready to step in, as was the case in Ghana and Nigeria, to assume positions vacated by the former colonial power.

In Guinea, the real power rested, not with the Deputies of the National Assembly or the Cabinet members, but with the seventeen members of the National Political Bureau. I noted that Ismaël Touré and Louis-Lansana Béavogui were members of the Political Bureau. President Touré was the Secretary General and Saïfoulaye Diallo (President of the National Assembly) was the Political Secretary of this all-powerful body. Despite the continued conjecturing on the part of some observers in Guinea during the 1959–1961 period concerning possible differences between Sékou Touré and Saïfoulaye Diallo, and the possibility of the latter attempting to take over the leadership of the Government, I always felt that Diallo, with his Fulah tribal background and his admiration for the progress made by the Chinese Communists, neither was in the position nor had the charismatic qualities to draw to himself the kind of support necessary to depose Touré. In my estimation, Sékou Touré was the real leader in fact and in symbol. He had those magnetic qualities and that know-how which seized the imagination and drew people to him. Saïfoulaye Diallo was in fact and in practice a "number two" man who preferred to shine in Touré's reflected glory. I could not picture Diallo as the leader of the Republic of Guinea. I could have been mistaken, of course, but I believed that N'Famara Keita had more of the qualifications for following in Sékou Touré's footsteps than Saïfoulaye Diallo. Keita was strong, tough, durable, and unafraid. He served well in whatever niche he was placed and had real possibilities as a statesman. However, Sékou Touré, despite his lack of formal education, stood head and shoulders above his colleagues, and he was certainly the "number one" man as far as the women of Guinea were concerned.

The posts in the National Political Bureau were filled through an election conducted by the Guinean Democratic Party. Rivalry for these choice positions was very keen, for membership in the National Political Bureau not only placed one within the inner planning circle, but also gave one added prestige and power. I have indicated already that Béavogui and Ismaël Touré not only held ministerial posts but also were members of the Political Bureau. The same was true of N'Famara Keita. The Political Bureau included also the President of the Women's Organization, the Ministers of Tourism, National Education, Youth and Sports, and the State, the Governor of the Bank, the Mayor of Conakry, and the head of the Guinean Labor Union. It was not so much the position held that gave one entrée into the Bureau as it was the individual in question. For example, conspicuously absent from the Bureau were the Defense Minister Fodéba Keita, the Minister of the Interior, the Minister of Telecommunications, the Minister of Industry and Mines, and the Minister of Finances. This seemed to indicate that without some kind of following, without crowd appeal or political influence, a party member stood little chance of being elected to the Political Bureau.

I shall never forget one night in September 1959. President Touré, resplendent in a flowing white *boubou*, stood on the platform of the assembly hall of the Guinean Democratic Party and delivered a five-hour, nonstop report to the Fifth National Congress of the Guinean Democratic Party. Seats had been reserved for the diplomatic corps near the front of the hall, and once Touré began talking, there was no question of leaving the room for any purpose. No Western or Eastern diplomat would risk having his departure misinterpreted by Touré or the members of his Government. Even though Touré was a dynamic speaker and his French was excellent, it was still something of an ordeal to sit through his five-hour presentation. I know that I could never speak in public for that length of time, or if I did it would be only to punish my adversaries. This was one of the many occasions on which President Touré took pains to point out that the instrument for decision-making in Guinea was the Guinean Democratic Party itself. In the words of Touré:

> If we do not understand the important fact that behind the State, there is something higher which is the Party, we cannot comprehend the political significance of these provisions in the Guinean Constitution at all. It is because the Party assumes the leading role in the life of the nation that it has at its disposal all the powers of the nation. The political, judiciary, economic, and technical powers are under the control of the Democratic Party of Guinea. And, therefore, it is the Party which elects the Chief of State by means of universal suffrage.

Touré and his colleagues claimed that the political party carried out its role "democratically," since all levels of the population became involved in the process of reaching decisions through the Village Councils and the County Councils, organized by the people themselves. They felt that at this stage in the nation's development it could not afford the luxury of several political parties that would dissipate energies and promote divisiveness. They were quick to point out, when questioned about the rigid control of the one-party system, that such a system did not differ radically from the communalism of traditional Africa, in which any opposition that might exist occurs within the party. Once there had been full discussion of an issue, and the issue had been decided, it was taken for granted that such a decision would be rigidly enforced, and no further discussion was in order.

Touré and his colleagues did not attempt to conceal the objectives of the political party to re-educate the people of Guinea, prevent disorder, and maintain unity in all echelons. They did not publicize the fact, however, that the Political Bureau was committed to take harsh action against those who spread dissension and threatened party unity. I had grave doubts concerning these claims about the democratic role of the Democratic Party of Guinea.

I could not conceive how it was possible to maintain that the Guineans were permitted to discuss matters frankly and openly and to engage in self-criticism if at the same time they ran the risk of being considered sowers of dissension. I wondered about the amount of freedom Guineans actually could

124

have with such absolute authority vested in a relatively small group, and I questioned what might happen to personal liberty in moments of crisis. The handling of the investigation and the conviction of those accused in May 1960 of trying to overthrow the Guinean Government bore out my misgivings about personal liberty under the one-party system.

Many problems beset President Touré and the members of his Government when they took office after the rupture with France. Guinea lacked trained economists, and Touré was the first to admit that his country's richness in agricultural and mineral resources meant nothing unless it would be possible to secure the technical know-how, financial assistance, and suitable markets to exploit these resources. More than 90 per cent of the people were untrained and illiterate, and there were many unemployed. The Guinean leaders, by their own admission, were immediately confronted with the perplexing problem of how to dispose of the bumper banana crop, harvested at the very moment in 1958 when the rupture took place between Guinea and France. The bananas were rotting on the piers of Conakry and Benty, and it appeared that the total crop was to be written off. The East Germans came up with an offer that was considered far from satisfactory by the Guineans; but under the circumstances the latter decided that this offer was preferable to dumping the bananas in the ocean. There was also the problem of disposing of the other main exports, coffee, pineapples, and palm kernels. Equally troublesome was the necessity of seeking new sources of basic foodstuffs such as rice, wheat, and sugar, sorely needed by the populace. Contrary to the rosy pictures painted by Guinean leaders, they were in trouble.

Immediately after the achievement of independence, the Guineans momentarily enjoyed unbridled feelings of elation at the thought that they had at last thrown off their "shackles of colonial bondage." They thought that they saw ahead a broad highway leading directly into an era of peace and freedom, in which it was going to be possible to enjoy the fruits of that independence so long denied to them and withheld from their grandparents and parents.

Great was the shock throughout Guinea when the discovery was made of the lengths to which General de Gaulle was willing to go to teach them what happened to those who were "ungrateful" for "all" that France had done for them. In keeping with De Gaulle's declarations concerning the fate in store for any territory that rejected the new Constitution and forfeited the right to enter the new French Community, the French Government had notified Guinea the day after the Constitutional Referendum that it was separated henceforth from the French Union. Although this notice of separation indicated also that French personnel serving in Guinea would be withdrawn—a serious blow to an emerging nation suffering from a dearth of trained technicians—its real significance lay in the fact that Guinea, as a free state, was no longer eligible to receive the financial aid and the administrative support supplied formerly by France.

Although President Touré and his Ministers never admitted it to me, they must have been somewhat dismayed at the abrupt cessation of French support, especially when they reminded themselves that 65 to 75 per cent of all Guinea's exports—agricultural and mineral— had gone to France. They were aware also that Guinea's foreign trade had been characterized by an excess of imports over exports, and that approximately 70 per cent of these imports had come from France. They knew, however, that Guinea had not appeared to suffer from this adverse trade balance in the franc zone. Guinea had received over a ten-year period approximately more than $75 million from FIDES (Fonds d'Investissement pour le Développement Économique et Social des Territoires) for the building and repair of bridges and highways; for enlarging the port in Conakry; for constructing schools and hospitals; and for improving agricultural production. Of course, the Guineans considered this money to be merely a return for the resources already contributed by Guinea to the French economy. But the severance of relations between their country and France meant that FIDES had been lost as a future source of funds.

When General de Gaulle had said that France would put no obstacle in the way of Guinea's independence, the Guineans did not interpret this to mean that France would refuse a helping hand to enable independence to become a reality. It is understandable that the Guinean Government, faced with possible economic collapse, accepted the skillfully couched barter trade agreements from the Communist bloc countries. The Government need not have been oriented toward the East to clutch at the well-aimed economic life preservers proffered by the Russians, the Czechoslovakians, the East Germans, and the Poles. In fact, I would suspect that many Guinean decisions made in the crucial days of newly won independence resulted from improvisation rather than a well-integrated master plan. The leaders had no time to size up these "saviors" from the bloc countries who rushed into their country swearing to save the "nonwhite downtrodden masses."

The Guineans were extremely conscious of and sensitive about the huge FRIA complex. This operation, with its bauxite mining and processing plant, represented the country's single largest manufacturing industry. But the Guinean leaders soon made the sorrowful discovery that this industry meant little to the new Government as a large source of revenue, since it was protected by a long-term agreement—drawn up while Guinea was still under French control—which barred any increase in export taxes. This long-term agreement became a bone of contention between Guinean officials and FRIA officials, and I became very much involved because of the large investment by Olin-Mathieson. My feeling was that this agreement should have been changed to give the Guinean Government a fairer share of the revenues, but I never expressed this opinion to the Guineans. I did make it known, however, to the French officials who were operating FRIA, and, to put it mildly, this suggestion was totally unacceptable.

The exploitation of the rich iron deposits eight miles north of Conakry by a French company, Compagnie Minière de Conakry, was no great source of comfort to the new Government other than that it employed a few Guineans; there was also a question as to whether this operation was to continue. My visit to the Los Islands, just off Conakry, to inspect the bauxite exporting operation carried on by a French company supported by Canadian capital, revealed that this operation was no great financial help to the Guinean Government, which sorely needed foreign currency. It was evident also that the mining of diamonds, which was just becoming important to Guinea, needed reorganization to put diamond smugglers out of business and to ensure the development of a legal market attractive to legitimate buyers. The Government was interested in reorganizing the diamond industry, but this was going to take time.

I saw some of the results of voluntary labor, euphemistically called by President Touré *investissement humain*. This labor had certainly cleaned and spruced up the city of Conakry. (Our chauffeur came running into the residence grounds one Sunday morning, however, and said that the youth group in charge of a work detail had tried to impress him into service. Their method of convincing him did not seem to allow any choice.) *Investissement humain* had supposedly accounted for the construction of 3,600 kilometers of new roads, hundreds of school classrooms, and many dispensaries, stores, and markets, the latter two of which did not begin to supply the needs of the economy.

So impressed with *investissement humain* was the French Socialist who drew up Guinea's first three-year plan—which, incidentally, proved most unsatisfactory—that he ventured to rely upon it for 20 per cent of a reported $120 million cost over a three-year period. It is little wonder that this plan faltered when put into effect, for it had assumed that approximately 70 per cent out of some two and one-half million people were going to work. This plan reputedly assumed that the rejection of what the Guineans called a "colonial economy" and the acceptance of a new economic structure (obviously socialist in concept) was going to enable Guinea to absorb within three years what some economists estimated to be investments totaling more than one-third of the estimated gross national product. I could well understand why the Government was so earnestly seeking, some three years later, the services of a well-known Harvard University lecturer who was an expert in developmental economics.

The sober confrontation with increasingly serious economic and social problems had caused even the most faithful and the most ardent members of President Touré's entourage to realize that it was going to take more than *investissement humain,* good intentions, long hours of work, and around-the-clock meetings of the National Political Bureau to put Guinea on the road to prosperity. I felt certain that these leaders had been forced to concede that a mere handful of men, no matter how deeply committed, had to look to the outside for advice and assistance when they lacked governmental experience and administrative expertise. On all sides I could see evidence that these men had learned the hard way what one writer has called the "great lesson of the twentieth century": "While it is possible to achieve political independence, complete economic independence is an impossibility." They had discovered that Guinean independence was going to become a myth unless they consented to do the very thing those Guineans, suffering from xenophobia, wanted least to do—look to foreigners for help and advice. It was this realization that had led the Guineans to open their doors to the Communist bloc after the French had closed off all avenues of help. The Communist bloc had counted on Guinea's need for economic and technical assistance.

The Western powers had ignored the realities of the situation and the urgency of the Guinean call for help. So the Western powers must share some of the responsibility for Guinea's early turn toward the East. And Western representatives should have felt a sense of guilt every time they stood viewing the scene and hypocritically wringing their hands in despair at the mounting evidence in 1959 and 1960 that the Communist bloc nations were using this new republic as a laboratory for determining the best methods of winning over the developing nations of Africa and striving desperately to make it their showplace.

Although the Communists had offered Guinea economic life preservers in the form of barter trade agreements, it was actually Prime Minister Kwame Nkrumah of Ghana who supplied the Touré Government with its first much-needed loan of $28 million. Nkrumah probably lived to rue the day that his generosity (or his Pan-African aspirations) persuaded him to extend this loan to Guinea, for he was still trying, in 1961, to put pressure on Touré to make interest payments on the loan in foreign currency. Touré wanted to pay off in Guinean francs.

The loan by Nkrumah was one of the results of the November 1958 provisional agreement that created the Ghana-

Guinea Union, which was finally sanctioned on May 1, 1959, during Nkrumah's visit to Guinea. The Soviet Union did not offer Guinea a $35 million line of credit until one month after my arrival in Guinea in 1959, and the Guinean Government did not accept this offer until March 1960 because it felt that the terms were too one-sided, with the advantage on the side of the Soviet Union. It was not until many months later that Communist China offered the Guinean Government a $25 million loan, supposedly interest free.

It was hard to see why the Guinean Government, in view of the size of the country and the already existing problems, accepted the recommendation—supposedly of a Czechoslovakian adviser—to create the Comptoir Guinéen de Commerce Extérieur to control the import of basic consumer goods and the export of agricultural products and mineral resources. I was certainly not at all surprised when some months later the responsibilities of the poorly functioning Comptoir Guinéen were handed over to the Ministry of Commerce, where they should have been in the first place. Guinean officials justified the existence of the Comptoir on the grounds that it ensured a constant flow of goods into the interior of Guinea at reasonable prices.

I always suspected that the Guineans would not have entered upon this venture if they could have foreseen how it was going to end. In my opinion, the big problem was in the operation of the Comptoir. Most of the people in charge were honest and conscientious, but they had no experience in buying or selling goods in large quantities. Furthermore, they had no idea about methods of getting goods to the places where they were most needed and when transportation was available. There were great losses in revenue from costly errors in purchasing more goods than needed, or goods that no customers wanted to buy.

I myself heard complaints from Guinean consumers who were disgruntled about their inability to secure rice, flour, sugar, and matches. I saw the empty shelves in the grocery stores before the Government attempted to set up co-operative stores. I myself bought sugar that did not melt in tea or coffee, and matches that did not light. I know that Guinean officials were most unhappy with the quality of goods imported in exchange for their bananas, pineapples, and coffee. I was told that Communist bloc countries were very dissatisfied because they did not receive from Guinea either the quantity or the quality of the agricultural products agreed upon. The disabled buses, jeeps, and cars that could be seen around Conakry and in outlying areas because parts could not be secured for them were stark testimony of the weakness of certain phases of the barter agreements. With the abolition of the Comptoir Guinéen, however, those people still trying to conduct private businesses in Guinea, who had been hampered by the restrictions of the Comptoir, began to see a faint glimmer of hope.

On March 1, 1960, I was summoned to the Présidence along with the rest of the members of the diplomatic corps, and with members of the press who happened to be in Guinea. It happened that Homer Bigart of *The New York Times* was visiting our Embassy on this day, and he went along with our USIS officer. Incidentally, I was called over to the Foreign

Ministry several days later and accused of making available the facilities of the Embassy to a newspaper reporter. What the angry Minister of Foreign Affairs was getting at was that Bigart needed an interpreter, and he concluded that the USIS man must have served in that capacity. If the USIS man did help Bigart out in this respect, he saw to it that I didn't know anything about it. I could, therefore, truthfully state that I was unaware that anything other than the usual courtesies had been extended to Mr. Bigart.

The President had called us together on March 1 to announce that as of that date Guinea was going to withdraw from the franc zone. We were quite surprised at this new development. For several months there had been rumors that Guinea might withdraw from the franc zone someday, but these rumors had not been taken very seriously. Touré pointed out that Guinea could never be completely independent without monetary reforms, because it was increasingly clear that the French banks still operating in Guinea were strangling the economy. Touré announced that the National Bank of Guinea had been created and within fifteen days all Guineans and other people residing in Guinea, regardless of nationality or diplomatic status, would have to replace all CFA francs with Guinean francs. In his best oratorical style, Touré pointed out that the Guinean currency was not tied to any other currency and that it was not going to be valid for export or for use in foreign trade.

Naturally, all of us were as concerned as the Guineans as to what was behind the Guinean franc, especially since President Touré had insisted that it was not tied to any foreign currency. This question became so pressing that the President found it necessary to try to answer it the following month (April 1960) at the National Conference of the Guinean Democratic party held at Kankan to discuss the Three-Year Development Plan. All of us in the diplomatic corps were invited to make the almost four-hundred-mile trip to Kankan as guests of the Government, in the small railroad coaches still in use. The Government had not yet secured the new diesel engine and cars from the Federal Republic of Germany.

At the Kankan Conference, President Touré told us that the foundation of Guinean currency was not some foreign currency or gold, but the national possessions of the country. He reminded us of the various units of monetary exchange used in Africa before the arrival of Europeans, and said that value had been determined by agreement supported by custom rather than by absolute standard. He declared that all loyal Guineans had faith in their national goods, and implied that others who were genuinely interested in the future of the nation had this same faith. He concluded by saying that he was removing the ever-present threat to Guinean sovereignty always inherent in a continuing tie-in with French finances.

Before we left Conakry for Kankan, we had seen tangible results of Guinea's withdrawal from the franc zone, for in addition to issuance of new Guinean franc notes bearing President Touré's picture, the former French Central Bank of Issue for the Federation of French West Africa had been turned into the main branch of the National Bank of Guinea. This new National Bank took over the handling of foreign currencies, and thus virtually put out of business the French banks still operating in Guinea. Its overbearing and difficult governor informed all Embassies that they would have to deal with the National Bank. There were wide repercussions to the withdrawal from the franc zone, and many of the problems created by this unheralded move had not been settled by the time of my departure from Guinea in March 1961.

The Government was also faced with the problem of what to do with former soldiers who had served with the French Army and were now returning in increasing numbers to Guinea with the hope of imposing special conditions for themselves upon the struggling Government. The unfortunate failure of Sylvanus Olympio, late President of Togo, to face up to this problem of the returning soldiers contributed in a large measure to his untimely death.

It was estimated that there were approximately 150,000 former soldiers in Guinea in 1959, and only five hundred had found employment in the Civil Service. The Government planned to interest the able-bodied veterans in serving in the Guinean Army with the understanding that they would be put to work building new roads, working on co-operative farms, and aiding in various government projects. President Touré revealed his political astuteness and statesmanship by carrying the problem of the returning soldiers directly to the Fifth Party Congress of September 1959. He disclosed this matter in the presence of the party members and of the diplomatic corps. Touré reported that he had heard that some of the veterans had vowed that if they could not find the kind of job opportunities they wanted, they were going to make trouble. Touré asked whether Guinean independence had been won by a handful of dissatisfied soldiers. He recalled that when they had been demobilized from the French Army while Guinea was under French rule, these veterans had never protested to the French Governor about employment, but had merely returned to their families to seek their former occupations or to cultivate the land. Touré said that these agitators would have gone over to the enemy if Guinea had been obliged to take up arms against France, since they would be on the side where the money was. He cited the example of the Chinese Communists who had fought for thirty-five years and had lost millions of supporters. He said that Chinese soldiers had returned to their former occupations or had become farmers; they had not all become civil servants. Touré said that many Guinean soldiers had been encouraged by outside forces to return to Guinea to make trouble. He appealed to the people to stick together, ignore the threats of dissident veterans, close ranks, and make the Guinean Democratic Party the leading influence in Guinea.

Few, if any, of those accused in May 1960 of plotting to overthrow the Government were former soldiers. Among the civilians condemned to death were a brilliant young Guinean lawyer, Ibrahima Diallo, and a religious leader, El-Hadj Mohammed Lamine Kaba, both of Conakry. In his May Day address, President Touré revealed to the populace and the diplomatic corps that a plot against his Government had been discovered and arms caches found at various points along the frontiers between Guinea and Senegal, and Guinea and the

Ivory Coast. In a frenzied speech Touré excoriated the sabo-
teurs and asserted that the guilty would be caught and given
the ultimate punishment.

Several days later Touré summoned the diplomatic corps
to the National Assembly chamber and gave us a lengthy
explanation of the crisis facing his Government. He told us
that the suspects would not be tried in the traditional courts
of Guinea, but would face a Popular Tribunal consisting of
members of the National Political Bureau, the Deputies of
the National Assembly, the members of the National Council
of the Guinean Labor Union, the members of the National
Council of the Youth Organization, and the Secretaries General of the three sections of Conakry. When I heard about the
size of this Popular Tribunal, and thought about the provoc-
ative nature of the radio broadcasts and the public statements already uttered by Sékou Touré himself, I wondered
just how much chance there was for the prisoners to receive
fair trials.

On May 4, 1960, we learned that a special committee appointed by an extraordinary Party Conference was to draw
up the dossiers of the accused, and the accused were to be
confronted by their accusers. On May 8 the members of the
Popular Tribunal met at 6:00 P.M. to hear the results of the
special committee's investigation and reach a verdict. Two
days later the verdict was announced. It was not possible at
any time between May 4 and May 8 to discover whether the
prisoners were defended by lawyers or given the opportunity
to appeal the verdict. All that the public knew was that
eighteen people were condemned to death—seven *in absentia*

(one of whom, a Frenchman, had escaped in a private plane); a French druggist was sentenced to twenty years at hard labor (released in 1961); a Swiss national received a sentence of fifteen years at hard labor (released in 1961); twenty-one Guineans were sentenced to five years at hard labor; and all those convicted had their property confiscated.

The diplomatic corps and the Guinean populace were very surprised to learn that Attorney Ibrahima Diallo and El-Hadj Mohammed Lamine Kaba had been accused of being agents working for a foreign power and sentenced to death. I did not know the religious leader, but I was acquainted with Diallo. I found it difficult to believe that he was in the employ of a foreign power. I did know that he was dissatisfied with the one-party system in Guinea and had openly discussed the possibility of organizing a second political party. He had made no effort to cover his dissent and had even discussed it at the April 1960 meeting of the party at Kankan. Diallo was intelligent and alert. Had he been working for a foreign power, he would have been clever enough to keep this hidden from his colleagues. I was aware that the religious leader Lamine had expressed dissatisfaction with the Guinean officials and had accused these officials of doing nothing for the masses, but merely looking out for their selfish interests.

The unfortunate part about this alleged coup is the fact that no outsiders were admitted to the trials or had access to the supposed evidence. It was never possible to determine whether the accused had been properly represented by counsel or given the opportunity to appeal the verdict. No announcement was ever made as to when, where, or how the death penalties were carried out. Nothing was ever done to refute the charges that the accused had been subjected to inhuman torture to induce confessions. Even in Algeria, the Ben Bella Government saw fit to announce when and how it executed those who plotted against the State. It was said in Guinea that secrecy had been necessary in order to avoid a tribal outbreak. As it was, secrecy merely evoked grave misgivings about the guilt of the accused.

In the second attempted coup of 1961, the major source of disturbance came seemingly from the youths and a few teachers (supposedly organized into a group or union) who accused the Guinean Government officials of having betrayed their trust and failing to achieve the goals set when independence was achieved. In this instance the Soviet Embassy in Conakry was accused by the Guinean Government of becoming involved with the Guinean Youth Organization, and the Soviet Ambassador was asked to leave Guinea toward the close of 1961. President Touré charged that Russian-trained or Russian-motivated Guineans had attempted to infiltrate not only the Youth Organization, but also the political and governmental structures. He declared that he did not intend to stand idly by while a foreign power directed the seizure of power from his hands. In this manner the honeymoon of Guinea and the Soviet Union was declared over, and Anastas I. Mikoyan was sent by Moscow to Conakry in an effort to salvage the Soviet position.

When I learned of the Soviet Ambassador's departure, I thought about the numerous times I had warned my Guinean counterpart and several of his colleagues that their certainty that President Touré and his Government would remain strong enough to withstand Communist infiltration tactics might well prove to be their undoing. Always they scoffed at the idea and called to my attention that the nearest Russian troops were thousands of miles away. I replied that I was not thinking about troops so much as about what would happen to Guinea if their Youth Organization, Women's Group, the Democratic Party of Guinea, and the various Ministries were successfully infiltrated. This could mean that one morning all of them might wake up to discover that they had to seek jobs elsewhere—that is, if they survived. The Guineans remained unimpressed by the Soviet record of imperialism in Eastern Europe, because they had the confidence that this could not happen to them so far from Moscow. They might have believed what President Touré often said jokingly, that he would accept help from the devil himself if it meant the saving of Guinea. But the devil always demands his pay.

Although a close lid of secrecy was clamped on the abortive coup in Guinea of November 1965, it was reported that President Touré accused France and the Ivory Coast of plotting his assassination. As a result of these accusations, France and Guinea recalled their ambassadors, and charges and countercharges were exchanged between officials of the Ivory Coast and of Guinea. This was not the first time Guinea and the Ivory Coast had been at odds, for I heard President Touré in December 1959 utter harsh charges against the Ivory Coast as well as against France. In 1965, however, the President of the Ivory Coast National Assembly charged Guinean police with extracting under duress a false confession from François

Camano, head of the Social Security Service of the Ivory Coast, who supposedly admitted over the Guinean radio that he had served as the agent of the Ivory Coast in a plot against President Touré. To complicate matters, the French police allegedly prevented Guinean agents from kidnaping and returning to Guinea the wife of a former Guinean diplomat. In view of the involvement of certain members of the French Secret Police in the disappearance in 1966 of the Moroccan Ben Barka, it was heartening to learn that the French police protected the wife of a former Guinean diplomat on French soil. Meager news reports from Guinea indicated that the chief protagonist in the 1965 plot was aided and abetted by at least two former government ministers, an army officer, and a number of small traders who belonged to an organization called the Parti de l'Unité Nationale de Guinée.

Whatever else these plots may mean, they indicate that Guinea, even seven years after independence, was still troubled with discontent and perhaps disillusionment over the failure on the part of the Touré Government to achieve some of the gains promised to the people in postindependence declarations.

VIII

Never a Dull Moment

Life was never dull during my tour of duty in Guinea, whether I was engaged in averting a break in diplomatic relations, representing the United States at the independence celebrations of newly emerging African nations, or supervising an airlift of Guinean soldiers in U.S. planes bound for the Congo.

One evening my neighbor, Ambassador Herbert Schroeder, called on me at the official residence prior to his return to Bonn, where he had been summoned by his Government. It was early in March of 1960, and the report was spreading throughout world capitals that the Republic of Guinea had become the first African nation to recognize the German Democratic Republic (East Germany). This report was supposedly based on pictures that had been made in East Germany purportedly showing the Guinean Ambassador to Moscow presenting his credentials to the East German President.

The Government of the Federal Republic of Germany

had been adhering to the Hallstein Doctrine, according to which it would sever diplomatic relations with any nation that recognized the Government of Communist East Germany. The calling home of Ambassador Schroeder on the heels of the news linking Guinea and East Germany seemed to be the first step in a break between West Germany and Guinea.

Despite the fact that no aid agreement existed between the United States and Guinea in March 1960, it was generally accepted among the Western and Eastern members of the diplomatic corps in Guinea that I had successfully established strong personal rapport with President Touré and the members of his Government. It was therefore not unusual for Ambassador Schroeder to seek my views in a moment of crisis. In addition, Ambassador Schroeder and I had established very friendly relations and often used our daily swim in the ocean to talk over mutual problems.

I told Ambassador Schroeder that nobody could advise him on a course of action and that he undoubtedly would have made his decision by the time of his arrival in Bonn. However, if I were in his place, I would, before leaving Conakry, send a message to my Government recommending that it investigate the incident carefully before taking any action as drastic as severing diplomatic relations with Guinea. I pointed out to Ambassador Schroeder that his country was the only Western power doing anything tangible toward making Guinea viable and it would be a tremendous blow to have this assistance cut off. I reminded him that the Guinean Government had resisted the efforts of the East German Trade

Mission in Conakry to establish an embassy, and I thought it significant that this report of the establishment of diplomatic ties between Guinea and East Germany had come at a time when President Touré was away from Conakry visiting his constituents in the brush. I assured the West German Ambassador that I would call unofficially on the Guinean Government to urge that every possible step be made to clear up this misunderstanding; until I was presented with specific proof that Guinea had taken the action claimed by East Germany, I intended to act as if the report were not true. We agreed, of course, that if Guinea actually had recognized East Germany, nothing could avert a break between his country and Guinea.

In keeping with my promise to Ambassador Schroeder, I called the next day on Acting President Abdourahmane Diallo, Minister of State, who happened also to be one of my neighbors in Donka. Diallo, never without his pipe, received me at the Présidence, and we immediately got to the matter at hand. I told him that I was there unofficially as a friend of the court and wished to stress the seriousness of the situation confronting Guinea in its relationship with the Federal Republic of Germany. I said that it would probably be the responsibility of the Guinean Government to take the initiative to establish beyond the shadow of a doubt what a Guinean diplomatic representative was doing in East Germany, if he had been there at all. Guinea must do this if it wished the community of nations to continue to believe its professed policy of positive neutralism and its affirmed belief in self-determination.

145

Acting President Diallo thanked me for my interest and said that to the best of his knowledge the Republic of Guinea had not recognized the East German Government. He admitted that the East German representative of the Trade Mission in Conakry had made repeated efforts to get the mission raised to the status of an embassy, but the Guinean Government had refused this. The Acting President said that he did not have the full details of the Guinean Ambassador's visit to East Germany, but he felt certain that it had nothing to do with the establishment of diplomatic relations. He assured me that word had been sent to President Touré to return to Conakry, and that the matter would be taken up with the President the moment he returned.

I expected that there would be increasing sentiment among certain government agencies in Washington to press for a break in diplomatic relations between the United States and Guinea, in order to present a united front with West Germany and to chastise Guinea for its failure to adhere to its policy of positive neutralism. I feared that such an action on the part of the United States would strike a fatal blow to American influence in Africa. West Germany itself had not formally broken ties with Guinea; it had merely called home its Ambassador for consultation. If the matter were settled in a satisfactory fashion between West Germany and Guinea, the United States, once it had broken, would find itself in an untenable position. Only as a last resort should a major world power break relations with a struggling developing nation that has yet to acquire skill and sophistication in things diplomatic. I planned and launched a campaign to combat any attempt to initiate a break between Guinea and the United States.

After a week went by and the Federal Republic of Germany had yet to report that it was going to break with Guinea, I began to feel slightly more at ease. President Touré returned to the capital and finally yielded to the insistence of the West German Government and answered several specific questions concerning the relation between the Republic of Guinea and the Communist East German regime. President Touré authorized his Ministry of Foreign Affairs to inform me that his answers to these questions were to be hand-carried to Paris, where they would be delivered to the West German Government by the Guinean Ambassador to France, Nabi Youla.

In the final stages of negotiations between Guinea and West Germany, West German officials came to Guinea during the first week of April 1960 and traveled to Kankan in Upper Guinea to have talks with President Touré, who was presiding over the National Conference of the Parti Démocratique de Guinée. Shortly after this discussion at Kankan, it became known officially that East Germany was not opening an embassy in Conakry and that there was not going to be a break between West Germany and Guinea.

Before Ambassador Schroeder returned to Guinea, his Government had requested the State Department in Washington to convey to me its warm thanks for the very helpful role I had played during a period of crisis between Bonn and Conakry. Upon the return of Ambassador Schroeder to Guinea, his first official act after his protocol visit to the Guinean

147

Ministry of Foreign Affairs was to come to my office in Conakry to express to me in person the thanks of his Government for my good services. This was one of the few moments during my stay in Guinea when I felt that my efforts had not been in vain.

Not long after the solution of the West German-Guinean *malentendu,* I received word from the State Department that I had been designated by President Eisenhower to be one of the representatives, with the rank of Special Ambassador, to attend the ceremonies at Léopoldville, in connection with the independence celebration of the Democratic Republic of Congo, scheduled for the last three days of June 1960. I was pleased with the assignment and looked forward to visiting this republic which had been granted its independence so suddenly by the Belgian Government after a somewhat confused "round-table" conference in Brussels. I was happy also at the prospect of renewing my acquaintance with former Undersecretary of State for Political Affairs Robert Murphy, who was to head the American delegation to the Congo.

It will be recalled that Mr. Murphy had presided over the meeting held at the State Department in the fall of 1959 during the state visit of Sékou Touré. Mr. Murphy had been very helpful to me in ironing out certain troublesome last-minute details. (Several of my academic colleagues have recently called to my attention the omission of my name from the list of delegation members attending the Congolese independence celebration, which appeared in Mr. Murphy's book *Diplomat Among Warriors.* I pointed out that this was an unfortunate oversight, since I was the only member of that delegation who was an accredited U.S. Ambassador to an African nation, and that mine was not the only name omitted, because Mr. Murphy had forgotten to mention the name of a very prominent Washington businessman who was most certainly a member of that delegation.)

My experience in Guinea made me wonder how the Congolese experiment was going to work out. I was concerned with the possible implications of the policy of the Belgian Government in limiting opportunities for higher education to only a very few Congolese. The Belgians had thought, in all probability, that their policy had prevented the awakening of "false" hopes in the minds of the great mass of Congolese, who then remained more easily manageable. Under the French regime Guinea had been far from the top of the list of territories from which students could go to France for advanced study. Yet I had reason to believe that even Guinea had had more students trained abroad than had the Congolese. If the Guinean Government was experiencing so much difficulty in maintaining its sovereignty and its independence, how could the Congolese Government expect to be better off when the Belgians moved out? At this particular stage the Belgians might have been lulled into thinking that their continued presence in the Congo was an absolute must; for, they thought the Congolese would fail miserably without Belgian technical and administrative skills.

Mr. Murphy has reported correctly that there was a mood of hope in the Congo before and during the independence celebration, but I personally found it extremely difficult to accept this hope, especially after having lived in Guinea for eleven months. Furthermore, I was unwilling to discount the serious disturbances among the rival political and tribal groups in the Congo, which had the earmarks of a nascent uprising. What was clear before independence and became increasingly clear after independence was that its leaders, Kasavubu and Lumumba, were pulling in opposite directions. This had not been the case in Guinea on the eve of independence. Moreover, it was well known even outside the Congo that Kasavubu was more the Belgians' choice than Lumumba, who was a veritable thorn in the Belgians' side. It interested me that the Guineans were so intensely for Lumumba, and I went to the Congo with the resolve to observe both these leaders closely with the hope of gaining some insight into the Congolese future. Of course, I realized the impossibility of unraveling the complex Congolese situation during a three-day ceremonial visit. I did not have the foresight to anticipate, however, that a little more than one month later the Congo would be torn with strife and slaughter and Belgian nationals would be fleeing for their lives.

I had to fly from Conakry to Dakar to meet the Military Air Transport Service plane bringing the rest of the American delegation to the Congo. We reached the airport in Léopoldville the following evening not long after the arrival of the official party from Belgium, and there was a good deal of excitement and bustle. Among the Congolese officials on hand to greet us at the airport was Antoine Gizenga, whom I had seen in Guinea several months before, when he visited Conakry on the way back to Léopoldville from the Brussels "round-table" conference. At the moment when Gizenga was shaking my hand, a photographer's flash bulb popped, and I remarked jokingly to C. Vaughn Ferguson, Jr. (later appointed Ambassador to the Malagasy Republic and one of the few really knowledgeable career officers in African affairs), that I wondered what State Department officials would have thought about my being in such a picture two or three months before.

There were no visible signs of the uneasy state of affairs that had preceded independence, and the Belgian Government had gone to great lengths to prepare an impressive series of inaugural events—receptions, dinners, luncheons, parades, cultural events, and fireworks.

I was particularly well received by Congolese officials, which I attributed to my being accredited to the Government of the Republic of Guinea, and to the high regard Lumumba and other Congolese had for President Touré. Some officials told me very frankly that they had never before seen a U.S. Ambassador who was a Negro.

I noticed that the name of Lumumba was conspicuously absent from the list of those participating in the solemn ceremony of granting and accepting Congolese independence. Indeed, the omission of his name made more of an impact than if it had been printed in bold letters. Nevertheless, as Delegate William Paley, board chairman of CBS, and I sought seats in the crowded and impressively new Parliament Chamber, we had no inkling of the real drama that would be played on that platform, where we saw King Baudouin and the Belgian and Congolese Ministers quietly awaiting the opening of the morning program (June 30).

King Baudouin, as was to be expected, made a brief, polite,

and tactful statement relinquishing his authority to rule the Congo, and granting full independence to the former territory. President Kasavubu, with a grace that momentarily diverted attention from his somewhat short and plump figure, accepted the authority on behalf of his Republic in a tempered and well-delivered speech of acceptance.

Thinking the ceremony about over, William Paley had just turned to say something to me when we both saw a tall, thin, ebony-hued young man get up from his seat on the platform and rush toward the microphone. When I saw the goatee I knew that this was Lumumba. The Congolese Prime Minister, who had been left out of the morning ceremonies, launched into a vitriolic attack on the Belgians, citing the wrongs and injustices inflicted upon the hapless Congolese during the Belgian occupation. Lumumba had seized the initiative in this solemn moment and was announcing to the world that he could not be silenced through the subterfuge of omitting his name from the program. To say that Lumumba's precipitous action caught everybody by surprise—Congolese, Belgians, visiting African dignitaries, Americans—would be an understatement. All of us looked to see whether the King and his Ministers were going to leave the platform in protest. Although the King's feelings were clearly visible, and his Ministers made no effort to conceal their anger and shock, no Belgian moved. The hush which had first descended over the audience was broken by hearty applause from Lumumba's followers. Lumumba, the wily, ruthless, fiery politician, was playing to the grandstand, but he was also making his bid for power; and it was evident he was not wanting for followers, if the number of Congolese applauding had any significance.

Lumumba's action that morning revealed his lack of common sense, propriety, timing, and judgment. Many Congolese and Belgians felt that their family squabbles should be settled behind closed doors, not aired in public before invited guests. The Prime Minister's act brought to the surface the instability and rashness which would be his undoing. It warned all those within hearing that here was a man who was going to be dangerous in the infighting and who would not hesitate to go for the jugular. Yet Lumumba, lashing out in some of the most bitter French I have ever heard, expressed the hidden sentiments not only of some of the Congolese listeners, but also of some of the visiting African dignitaries, as he castigated the Belgians for their "exploitation" of the defenseless Congolese and for their "avariciousness."

As Lumumba turned from the microphone, the session broke up amid the loud buzzing of excited voices. Outside the Parliament Chamber I saw a crowd collecting around Lumumba, and soon heard the angry, agitated voices of Congolese Ministers, all trying to speak at once. This noise did not subside until a Belgian, accompanied by a Congolese official, approached the group and spoke a few words. The crowd dispersed, and order reigned once again.

At the crowded luncheon following the tension-packed morning session, a hush once again swept over the guests when Patrice Lumumba got up to speak. I looked at him and wondered what else he could possibly have to say. I had underestimated Lumumba's versatility and his ability to change positions. Speaking in tones no longer strident, and wearing a somewhat subdued air, Lumumba proceeded to sing the praises of those whom he had condemned one hour ago. He cited the constructive things done by the Belgians during their regime in the Congo and concluded his startling remarks with the hope that co-operation and understanding between the Congolese and the Belgians would continue after independence.

I left the table immediately and went in search of a Congolese official whom I had met in Conakry several months before. I asked him to explain this bewildering conduct. The official was reluctant to talk. He hastily explained, however, that the Belgian Ministers had told Lumumba and the Congolese Ministers that the King would leave Léopoldville that day if Lumumba did not retract his harsh accusations of the morning. Lumumba seemingly had found it difficult to understand what all of the fuss was about, for he had merely repeated what he had been saying for a long time across the length and breadth of the Congo. Lumumba overlooked the fact that formerly he had not been talking in the presence of the King, a captive listener, on the occasion of his surrendering a territory. Sékou Touré had likewise spoken out one day in the presence of a distinguished visitor, General de Gaulle; but on that August day in 1958, Touré had taken a calculated risk and had spoken from a well-prepared text, submitted in advance, so it is said, to the French Governor General of Guinea.

I did not react to Lumumba at all in the same fashion in

which I had reacted to Sékou Touré. Lumumba puzzled me, it is true, but he did not impress me. I respected Touré, but I could not bring myself to respect Lumumba. I might have had more respect for him if, despite his blatant show of poor manners and his lack of diplomacy, he had refused to recant and had stood by his bristling statement of the morning. Touré would not have recanted; he would have gone to perdition first. Naturally, I could understand how a politician, under pressure from the angry Belgian Ministers and his conciliatory Congolese colleagues, fearful that the King's departure would mar the celebration, might opt to compromise. But to recant publicly in such a humiliating fashion after exhibiting such defiance a short time before did not, in my opinion, engender respect.

Lumumba's exercise in poor taste and political expediency caused me to think back over the events of the two preceding days. I had been faintly aware that whenever King Baudouin appeared in public, President Kasavubu had always been at his side, engaging him in conversation. In each instance, Lumumba had been seated or standing off to one side. Every time a cameraman approached to photograph the King and Kasavubu, Lumumba had edged his chair over to get into the picture, or he had jumped out of his seat, rushed up to Kasavubu, and engaged his attention. This was not a matter of my imagination, because these maneuvers had been repeated too many times within forty-eight hours. I did begin to question how long a man with the drive, ambition, and *amour-propre* of Lumumba was going to allow himself publicly to be relegated to a secondary position. After all, Lumumba probably had a sense of history as well as an image of himself as a great leader.

There is little point in conjecturing about what might have happened if the Belgians and Congolese responsible for planning the celebration ceremonies had given a more prominent role to Patrice Lumumba in the hope of dissipating the intense rivalry smoldering between him and Kasavubu. This would have brought simply a temporary truce. The roots of the problem went much deeper, and the Belgians themselves must be held greatly responsible for subsequent events in the Congo. It is not necessary to hark back to the time of Leopold II, whose reign (1865–1909) was characterized by industrial and colonial expansion, and whose ruthless greed and condonation of very harsh treatment of the Congolese in the Congo Free States, then under his personal rule, provoked international protests which led to this area being ceded to Belgium in 1908. Nor is it necessary to discuss the Belgian-controlled Union Minière du Haut-Katanga, operating in the Katanga Province, that once produced most of the world's supply of cobalt, as well as quantities of uranium, radium, copper, tin, and diamonds. Small wonder that Moïse Tshombe could not resist the temptation to secede, with the Katanga Province as his base of operations.

The Belgians had not prepared the Congolese for self-rule. They had been satisfied to keep the situation under control by playing one tribal group against another. Many of the improvements in sanitation, roads, buildings, etc., came about as a result of creating more favorable conditions for the thousands of Belgian civil servants and business people living and working in the Congo. The French had done something somewhat similar in Guinea for the same reasons. When the freedom avalanche began to gain momentum in the Congo, the Belgians gave in to the pressures and stepped out, not in anger, as De Gaulle left Guinea, but in panic. The United Nations could not find a satisfactory solution to the mess which resulted from the poorly managed Belgian pull-out.

A sidelight to the visit of the American delegation to Léopoldville came as the result of a chance remark I had made to Minister Ismaël Touré, Guinean delegate to the Congolese independence celebration. During a luncheon I was seated with William Paley and saw the Minister and another guest looking for seats. I said jokingly to Mr. Paley that I was going to bring together a "Marxist-oriented" Guinean and a "big American" capitalist. I called to Minister Touré and his friend from the Cameroons and asked them to join us. I served as interpreter for what turned out to be a very enjoyable conversation. I told Minister Touré that I understood many delegates were having difficulty getting plane reservations out of Léopoldville, and if he ran into any trouble to let me know. I gave this conversation no further thought until Friday, July 1, at the parade, when the Guinean consul to Ghana came up to the reviewing platform and said that Minister Touré and he would appreciate getting a ride as far as Accra. I consulted with our delegation head, Robert Murphy, and he said he would be delighted to have the Guineans aboard. On Saturday, in addition to the American delegation, Minister Touré, the Guinean Consul, and two unexpected Ghanaian delegates boarded the American plane at the ultramodern Léopoldville Airport.

It had been previously decided that this MATS (Military Air Transport Service) plane was to land at Conakry instead of at Dakar to let me off, and I had persuaded the American delegation to come to the residence for light refreshments, to be followed by a quick tour of Conakry. I had sent ahead a wire to my new deputy, Tony Ross, to alert my wife so that food and drinks would be ready at the residence that afternoon. Once Minister Touré was aboard, I mentioned casually that the plane was going to land at Conakry, and that he would be welcome to go the full distance with us. He thanked me but declined the offer. The Minister's plan was to make connections with President Touré's plane, due in Accra that day.

We landed at Accra, and Minister Touré and the Consul departed with their baggage. I learned from American Ambassador William Flake, who met our plane, that President Touré's plane had left Accra that morning. Within a few moments Minister Touré reappeared alone, expressing apologies, and asked if he might accompany us to Conakry. I immediately wired ahead to Ross to let the Guinean Government know that Minister Ismaël Touré was returning with us. I also suggested that he invite all available Guinean Ministers and Western diplomats to the impromptu gathering at the residence.

As we circled over the Conakry Airport preparatory to making what was to be the first landing of an American plane on Guinean soil, I could see a large crowd assembled in front of the waiting room. With Minister Touré leading the way, we filed out of the plane to find all the Guinean Ministers and Western diplomats who were in or around Conakry that Saturday, waiting to greet the Minister and the visiting American dignitaries. At the entrance to the airport we found a long line of cars, with a police escort. The American delegation were assigned seats in cars with the various Guinean Ministers, and the procession made its way from the airport to the residence in Donka. After the brief reception we re-entered the cars, drove through the streets of Conakry and returned to the airport.

It should not be difficult to imagine the bewilderment, not only of my Western colleagues, but also of the Communist bloc diplomats, at the unaccustomed sight of Guinean Ministers and American visitors riding together through the streets of Donka and Conakry. With the slow pace and the open cars, there was no difficulty in seeing who was talking to whom. As somebody remarked, the United States got as much benefit and good will from bringing Minister Touré back from the Congo as it did from opening a cultural center in Conakry.

In November 1960 I was again designated by President Eisenhower to be a representative with the rank of Special Ambassador to an independence celebration. This time it was the celebration of the independence of the Islamic Republic of Mauritania, to be held at Nouakchott, beginning November 27. On this occasion the President sent just two of us, the other being Henry S. Villard, the American Ambassador at Dakar.

Ambassador Villard was sent as the President's personal representative, which meant that he was the ranking member authorized to convey to the Mauritanian President the congratulatory statement from the United States and the personal gift of President Eisenhower. The colorful ceremonies that took place in Nouakchott, a city that had been constructed literally in a portion of the desert, went off with a smoothness and precision that were indeed admirable. The speech turning over authority, delivered by French Minister Debré, and the acceptance speech by President Mokhtar Ould Daddah were well received by the Mauritanians and visitors. Feeding the more than a thousand visitors was a veritable *tour de force* made possible by supplies flown in from Dakar and France. The parade featuring Mauritanian paratroopers in camouflaged uniforms and soldiers in desert garb mounted on camels added to the exotic setting. The friendly and hospitable Mauritanians had the knack of making visitors feel welcome. I regretted very much when their first effort to enter the United Nations was thwarted. The Mauritanian Republic was finally admitted to the United Nations in 1961, despite the opposition of Morocco, which laid claim to a portion of its territory.

When I had returned to Guinea on July 2 from Léopoldville, aboard that United States plane with its efficient crew, I had no reason to believe that, within one month and a few days, I was to become the unwilling supervisor of an airlift involving United States planes flying under the flag of the United Nations. Not long after the Congolese independence celebration, civil strife had erupted in the Democratic Republic of Congo and had destroyed all traces of law and order.

The United Nations had intervened in the middle of July and authorized the establishment of a United Nations force that was to protect the Congo from foreign intervention and aid in the restoration of peace. Secretary General Dag Hammarksjold had appealed to member states of the United Nations to contribute troops to the United Nations force there. The Secretary General received pledges of troops from Guinea, Ghana, Ethiopia, Morocco, Tunisia, and the newly formed Mali Federation (which dissolved after 1960 because of political dissension and became the Republic of Senegal and the Republic of Mali).

I never discovered the real reason why Secretary General Hammarskjold did not accept immediately Guinea's pledge of troops, as he accepted the pledges of the other African nations. President Touré interpreted Hammarksjold's action as a reflection on Guinean national honor and challenged this failure to process Guinea's pledge in the same fashion as the pledges of other African states. The Secretary General then acknowledged acceptance, but indicated that the Guinean troops would be called up at a future date and might be used for police duty. Touré then issued an ultimatum to the United Nations which said in effect that if the United Nations did not offer immediately to put Guinean soldiers to an honorable use in the Congo along with the troops from other African nations, his Government intended to place these troops directly at the disposal of the Government of the Democratic Republic of Congo. The United Nations re-

161

sponded swiftly to the Touré threat, and this decision led to "Operation Airlift."

In the latter part of August I was informed that American planes flying under the flag of the United Nations were going to arrive in Guinea within the next twenty-four hours to begin the airlift of troops to the Congo. I did not feel that this information presented any immediate problems to our Embassy, since the operation was to be under the supervision of the United Nations Mission in Conakry assigned to aid the Guinean Government develop administrative cadres. Naturally, our personnel would co-operate in every way possible, but this was a United Nations operation. The United States and other powers had merely offered to give help in the form of transportation, communications, and supplies.

The United Nations Mission in Conakry received word that a U.S. Air Force officer, in charge of the logistics of the airlift, was to arrive on a plane coming from the American air base in Châteauroux, France. Merely as a courtesy gesture, I was on hand at the airport to greet the officer when he arrived several hours later in a huge C-119 transport plane. Major Behrens had expected to load the plane immediately with soldiers and supplies, but discovered that the first contingent from the interior had not arrived at the airport. A hasty consultation brought the decision to postpone the departure until the following day.

The next morning the Guinean troops were assembled in the center of Conakry near the political party headquarters. President Touré made a brief speech urging the troops to comport themselves as brave men and to fight to liberate their

African brothers in the Congo. He then asked Major Behrens to stand at his side as the troops passed in review and marched to the buses and trucks waiting to carry them to the airport. The members of the Guinean Government then hurried to the airport to see the take-off. Theirs was a long wait because the food supplies and military equipment had to be loaded first. There was some question about the weight of this matériel as a steady stream of soldiers carried it into the yawning opening at the rear of the C-119. The President and his Ministers were becoming somewhat impatient at the unforeseen delay, but finally the soldiers assigned to take off in the first contingent were aboard.

I had been standing near the C-119, watching the loading operations, when suddenly I heard my name called. As I turned around, I saw the Embassy political officer, John Cunningham, hurrying across the tarmac in the morning heat. Cunningham, called "Pat" by all of us at the chancery, was perspiring heavily by the time he reached me, and I could see that he was very much troubled. In his hand were two telegrams, and when he handed them to me he said softly: "Mr. Ambassador, here are two more problems for your attention."

The telegrams had not been sent to me, but were directed to Major Behrens and the captain of the C-119. They had been sent in my care from Châteauroux through commercial channels, which meant that anybody in the downtown telegraph office in Conakry who could read English already had had access to their contents. The stark, succinct messages typed on those yellow slips of paper indicated that the airlift had been suspended and that the captain of the C-119 was ordered to return immediately to the air base at Châteauroux.

Cunningham stood by in silence as I glanced hurriedly at the dismaying words. Without a word to him, I placed the telegrams quickly in my inside coat pocket, walked over to the major and captain and said: "Come on, men, let's get this blooming plane out of here before Thanksgiving Day finds us still trying to get to the Congo." My tone was quiet, and I was not smiling. The captain saluted smartly, thanked us for our hospitality, climbed into the plane and started the engines. He taxied the huge plane off the tarmac toward the airstrip as the military band struck up the Guinean national anthem. The members of the Government were waving good-bye. After a brief warm-up, the C-119 started down the runway with its very heavy load, and as it approached the end of the runway it still was not airborne. At that moment the terrible thought passed through my mind that possibly the runway was not long enough for a plane so heavily laden to get off the ground in the heat of the day. Seemingly with inches to spare, the plane with its precious cargo lifted off the ground, wavered just for a moment and rose toward the noonday sun.

As the plane disappeared in the distance, I turned to the major and said, "Major, I have just done something which is probably going to cause all hell to break loose, but I want you to know that I stand ready to accept the sole responsibility for my act."

The major was clearly surprised by what I had said, but he waited with quiet interest for what was to follow.

"Did you see the two messages which FSO Cunningham delivered to me a short while ago? What I mean to say is, did you see him hand me two yellow slips of paper?"

"As a matter of fact I did, Mr. Ambassador, and I was wondering whether or not something important had come up about our air operation."

"The truth is that something very important has come up which is going to complicate life for us here in Guinea for the next forty-eight hours or so." I gave him the two telegrams, which he proceeded to study carefully. It was not until after I saw the faint traces of a smile beginning to form on the major's features that I began to feel a little more hopeful about the whole business.

"Major," I continued, "I had to withhold those messages from you and the air force captain, for once you had seen them you would have had to comply. I'm sure that you can understand that I would rather have faced a firing squad than have been forced to go up in that airport balcony to tell President Touré, Defense Minister Fodéba, and their colleagues that the airlift was off. What explanation could I have offered?"

"You were confronted with a tough decision, Mr. Ambassador, and you have undoubtedly made it on the basis of your knowledge of the situation here."

"Can you imagine yourself, Major, going into that plane to tell those soldiers to get off the plane, unload the supplies and munitions, and await orders to return to their encampment? How do you suppose they would have reacted, especially those who are obviously none too military? What would have been the reaction of that huge crowd of Guineans massed around the airport to see the triumphal departure of the first contingent of troops ever to leave the Republic of Guinea?"

After reiterating that I was accepting full responsibility for withholding the two official messages, and stood ready to be recalled for so doing, I went on to explain that I had had no alternative. It was my feeling that, if the orders had been carried out as directed, the United Nations as well as the United States would have been in a position not only delicate but untenable. I said that there had already been enough problems concerning Guinean troops going to the Congo without the United States taking any unilateral action that could be interpreted as blocking their passage. I requested the major's assistance in demanding the reason why the airlift was called off and in urging that the operation not be suspended but carried out in keeping with the U.S. pledge to the United Nations. The major consented to help.

We sent messages to Washington and to Châteauroux, and had the local UN Mission send one to New York, insisting on an explanation for the cancellation of the airlift and stressing the necessity of keeping the promise to transport Guinean troops to the Congo. Then began one of the most tedious waits of my stay in Guinea.

The Guinean Government had been informed that the schedule for the arrival of the next plane was somewhat uncertain, but word was supposed to come confirming the arrival time.

A 8:00 P.M. the same day the telephone rang at the residence, and I recognized the voice of Minister Fodéba Keita. He asked me when the airlift was to recommence. I reminded him that this was actually an operation by the United Nations, and I did not know exactly when the next plane would reach Conakry. The Minister informed me that if no American planes had arrived by the next day, the Government would have to seek its own mode of transportation to the Congo. These words brought to my mind a picture of IL-18's with Czechoslovakian pilots coming in from Accra to pick up the stranded Guinean soldiers.

I did not sleep well that night, and found no difficulty in getting up at 4:30 A.M. when a ringing telephone added its noise to that of the heavy rainfall outside. An unfamiliar voice said that the caller was the airport commandant and that he wished to speak to the American Ambassador. I asked him what he wanted. He said he had been instructed to call me because an American plane was asking permission to land at the airfield. He could not grant permission unless the American Ambassador himself certified the permission to land. I told the commandant that the airlift was an operation of the United Nations. The United States had assigned these planes to the UN to be flown under the flag of the United Nations. The commandant said his instructions were that 1 had to certify the permission to land. I gave the commandant my word that I would come to the airport, and told him if another plane came over requesting permission to land to let it come in. I also told him to call Minister Fodéba Keita and ask him to meet me at the airport. I called my deputy, Tony Ross, and asked him to meet me at the airport within the next hour. I also called Major Behrens at the Hôtel de France and asked him to come to the airport.

167

It was still raining very hard when I left the residence, and dawn had not broken. I reached the airport first, and the saluting guards informed me that the commandant was upstairs in the restaurant with some Americans. Standing in the door of the restaurant with a crew of young American pilots was the somewhat upset airport commandant, who could speak no English. He smiled with relief as I approached. The captain of the American plane stepped forward and in a broad southern accent told me that he surely was glad to see me. He explained that a number of C-130's had landed at Dakar. One plane had continued on to Conakry, arriving there at 1:00 A.M., but had not been given permission to land. It was decided in Dakar that the difficulty was due to a misunderstanding, because the person in the tower had not spoken English clearly enough. (Under the terms of a United Nations agreement, a Czechoslovakian national was working in the tower at the Conakry airport.) The next plane sent in had a French-speaking American aboard, and it had received permission to land. I discovered that the airport at Conakry had not been equipped for night landings, and this American plane had come into an unfamiliar airfield during a rainstorm by means of the plane's landing lights and some flares set up by the Guineans on the airfield.

I then learned that the telegrams from Châteauroux, announcing the suspension of the airlift, had failed to say that this delay was only temporary. Someone at that air base had discovered that the airport's runway was not long enough for heavily loaded C-119 planes to take off with safety. The order had been given to take C-119's out of the operation and replace them with C-130's, which could take off fully loaded after a very short run. Nobody had thought of notifying Conakry that there had been a change in plans or that there would be at least a thirteen-hour delay while sufficient C-130's were called in to carry on the airlift.

By this time Minister Fodéba Keita had arrived in very good humor at the prospect that the airlift would go on. He ordered breakfast for the American crew, Major Behrens and his staff, and for Ross and me. He said that arrangements had been made for meals to be served to all American airmen who would arrive during the next two days. The crews staying overnight (night flying was not possible) would be kept at the Hôtel de France as guests of the Government. He apologized for my having been called to the airport through a misunderstanding, but said that the commandant had been unaware that the landing permission secured for the C-119 planes applied to any planes that might be used to airlift Guinean troops to the Congo.

I did not let the Guinean Minister know just how happy I had been to see that C-130 crew and to learn that the airlift would go on. It was indeed an inspiring sight to see the plane take off soon afterwards with its load of soldiers and supplies. The arrival and the departure of these planes at two- or three-hour intervals continued for the next two days. All plane traffic was stopped after 5:00 P.M., and the last crew to arrive went into Conakry to enjoy a good meal at the Hôtel de France. One plane developed engine trouble, necessitating the flying in of a new engine a day later from an air base in Morocco. An around-the-clock guard of Guinean soldiers watched over the plane until it was repaired. The installation of the engine was watched with avid interest by the soldiers and airport personnel, for this was a most unusual operation in this section of Africa.

During the afternoon of the first day of the arrival of the C-130's, President Touré and his Ministers arrived at the airport with General Diane Lansane, a member of the National Political Bureau who had been promoted to the rank of General at the beginning of the Congo crisis. The General and his staff went aboard the waiting C-130 after a brief ceremony.

When the last Guinean contingent had been flown from the Conakry Airport, I was able to breathe more easily. I could truthfully express sincere thanks for the United States Air Force, even though the planes had been flying under the UN flag. I knew that the Eastern Communist members of the diplomatic corps had spent a very uneasy forty-eight hours, during a goodly portion of which American planes had been in the Guinean skies.

In addition to the satisfaction of seeing this efficiently carried-out operation—once it had got under way—was the satisfaction of receiving a letter from the Chief of Staff of the United States Air Force, Thomas D. White, congratulating me for what he called the "inspired, split-second decision . . . to continue the airlift when it had apparently, but mistakenly been cancelled."

IX

Guinea: Crossroads of Sub-Saharan Africa

Guinea became something of a crossroads in sub-Saharan Africa from the moment it achieved its independence. It became also a meeting place for those Africans who were dissatisfied with the slow progress toward freedom in their homelands. At a given point in time it was often possible to see at the Hôtel de France or in the streets of Conakry dissidents from the Cameroons, the Ivory Coast, Portuguese Guinea, Angola, Ghana, Algeria, and many other places.

Along with his pressing duties as President, Sékou Touré had to play host to numerous dignitaries, among whom could be counted President William Tubman of Liberia, Prime Minister Kwame Nkrumah of Ghana, President Modibo Keita of the Republic of Mali, President Sukarno of Indonesia, Prime Minister Patrice Lumumba of the Democratic Republic of Congo, President of the Presidium of the Supreme Soviet Leonid I. Brezhnev, and Marshal Tito of Yugoslavia. I witnessed the arrival and participated in the activities that went on during these visits. Unfortunately for me, Marshal Tito did not visit Guinea until after I had returned to the United States. It was rumored while I was in Guinea that Khrushchev was going to visit this African republic, but the visit never took place, either during my stay in Guinea or after my departure.

There was such a constant coming and going of delegations that I wondered how officials in this new nation facing the difficult problems confronting their Government found it possible to play host to so many people. It was not just that these visits consumed much valuable time and energy, but they must have been quite costly. A rich nation like the United States has sought ways and means of shortening and simplifying state visits without detracting from the purpose or the importance of such visits.

The most significant visits to Guinea during my tour of duty there were those made by Lumumba, Nkrumah, Keita, and Brezhnev. I have not singled out these visits because of their great pomp and ceremony, for these elements were a part of all visits of dignitaries to Guinea. They were important in my estimation either because of the joint communiqués issued at their conclusion, speeches made during the visit, or incidents that occurred.

Since I had got down to Léopoldville during the Congolese independence celebration and had seen Lumumba in action, I wanted to see how he would perform in the first French-speaking republic in West Africa to win its independence from France. I found it difficult to understand how Lumumba was willing to leave the Congo in the midst of the uprising which was bringing death and untold misery to Congolese and Belgians alike, visit the United Nations, and then stop off for a series of visits in North and sub-Saharan Africa. Lumumba used as his reason for going to New York the necessity of pleading his cause in person at the United Nations. After his appearance at the UN, the Congolese Prime Minister saw Premier Habib Bourguiba of Tunisia (August 3, 1960), and on the next day went to see King Mohammed V of Morocco and his son Crown Prince Moulay Hassan (who became King of Morocco after his father's death in 1961). After visiting Guinea (August 6–7), Lumumba went to see Liberian President William Tubman (August 7), and ended his visits with a call on Prime Minister Nkrumah of Ghana. There was some question in my mind about the judgment of a leader who felt that he could spend that much time away from his people in a period of crisis. Lumumba was actually appealing to his fellow Africans for aid to ensure his personal victory in the Congo.

The singular feature about the Lumumba visit to Guinea was the number of times those of us in the diplomatic corps had to journey to the airport to welcome a plane that had not even left Morocco. Between 12:00 noon, Friday and 2:30 A.M., Saturday we were summoned to the airport three times by the Guinean Protocol Chief only to discover upon reaching the airport that Lumumba's plane had not arrived. It was never admitted that the plane had delayed its take-off from Morocco because of some mechanical defect. Aside from the inconvenience and the vexation of riding back and forth in the heat, however, we did not fare as badly as the inhabitants of Donka and Conakry, many of whom stood for hours along the airport route to welcome the fiery Congolese leader.

On my final trip out to the airport in the driving rain of

the early morning hours of that August Saturday, I could hear the shouts of the police and members of the Youth Organization, who were silhouetted in the beams of the automobile headlights as they roused the sleeping inhabitants and directed them to return to the parade route to welcome Lumumba.

Lumumba's plane finally did land, and the ebullient and not easily nonplussed Protocol Chief, Sassone, moved forward to introduce the African leader to a weary and somewhat sleepy diplomatic corps. Not even Ambassador Knap of Czechoslovakia could muster up his usual show of cordiality and enthusiasm. All of us returned to the Présidence with President Touré, Lumumba, and his large delegation. We sipped champagne or fruit juice, and then disappeared into the night to salvage what was left of it.

That next afternoon I returned to Conakry to hear Lumumba address the people from a platform which had been constructed in front of the Présidence. The streets around the Présidence were crowded with people waiting to hear the speech over the public address system. Since there was no King Baudouin on the platform in Conakry that afternoon, Lumumba did not have to be so careful of what he said. He used the same fighting language employed during his unheralded appearance at the independence ceremony in the Congo in June. He attacked the "imperialistic" Belgians and the "other imperialistic forces" that, according to him, were trying to "besmirch the hard-won Congolese independence." Lumumba was spurred on by the vigorous applause of his Guinean audience and bloc diplomatic members. He accused UN Secretary General Dag Hammarskjold of failing to play his role in the Congo. He challenged Hammarskjold to explain why the United Nations force was parading in certain parts of the Congo, but not in Moïse Tshombe's Katanga Province. He accused the Belgians of merely seeking a pretext to return to the Congo to finish their exploitation of this part of the continent. He proclaimed loudly that the Congolese were going to refuse all "imperialist aid" and were not going to become a colony of the United Nations.

Lumumba was at his crowd-stirring best. None of us in the audience had reason to suspect that this was the last time he would be seen or heard in Guinea. The spectre of death did not seem to be hovering around the tall young revolutionary, whose failing was not knowing when to begin to build constructively after having fought for and won a cause.

Lumumba went to some lengths to emphasize his personal efforts to secure Congolese unity, and he stressed the necessity for African unity also. He told us that Bourguiba, Mohammed V, and Sékou Touré had assured him the help of their respective nations, and he declared that he intended henceforth to disregard the United Nations force and call directly upon Africans for aid in the fight for Congolese independence.

After his speech and ride through the streets of Conakry in President Touré's open Cadillac, followed by a bus bearing Guinean Ministers and members of the diplomatic corps, Lumumba returned to the Présidence for deliberations with Touré and his Ministers.

Not until I saw the joint statement issued at the end of the visit did I have any inkling of the nature of the exchange

175

between the Guineans and the Congolese visitors. The statement, distributed to the press and the diplomatic corps, condemned the subversive action of "imperialistic Belgium" and its allies through armed aggression. It pledged aid in reestablishing peace and in safeguarding the territorial integrity of the Congo. It condemned the secession of Katanga Province from the Democratic Republic of Congo, and insisted that the UN Secretary General should send the UN force into Katanga without delay. Complete solidarity was expressed for the Algerian fight for independence, and "Apartheid" in South Africa was severely condemned. Compliance with the Charter of the United Nations was reaffirmed, and the belief was expressed that Africa could make a contribution to the world through positive neutrality and fraternal co-operation.

Lumumba's departure from Guinea went off smoothly, in sharp contrast to the hectic circumstances which had marked his arrival. All of Guinea was shocked and embittered when the news of Lumumba's assassination in the Congo the following January became generally known early in February. The Guinean populace had not reacted in this fashion even to the revelation some months earlier of the death of Dr. Félix Moumié, a Cameroons dissident, who had died in Switzerland from poison administered by an unknown enemy.

The next significant visit to Guinea, in December 1960, created much speculation and interest in the diplomatic corps because its purpose was the creation of a three-nation union. I have mentioned elsewhere the bonds existing between Ghana and Guinea resulting in the formation of the Ghana-

176

Guinea Union. I learned that a third African nation had decided to join the Union, and it was for this reason that Prime Minister Nkrumah and President Modibo Keita of the Republic of Mali journeyed to Guinea on December 22. They came to form the Ghana-Guinea-Mali Union.

I had met neither Nkrumah nor Keita, but I had been hearing about the former for a good many years before he became Ghanaian Prime Minister, because of his prominence in the Pan-African movement. Nkrumah's active interest in the Pan-African movement stemmed from the time he had served as secretary of the congress of Negro leaders held in Manchester, England, in October 1945. Nkrumah had been influenced in his thinking about Pan-Africanism by his close friend George Padmore of the West Indies and by Dr. W. E. B. DuBois, the brilliant and controversial American Negro leader. It had been Nkrumah, however, who persisted in the effort to get other African leaders to accept the idea of a Union of Independent African States.

Thirteen months before my arrival in Africa, Nkrumah had served as host to the first conference of Independent African States, held in Accra scarcely a year after Ghanaian independence. At the June 1959 meeting in Saniquelli, Liberia, neither Nkrumah nor Touré had been able to persuade the cagey elder statesman, William Tubman of Liberia, to join their Union. In fact, Tubman skillfully outmaneuvered these young leaders and gave them a lesson in statesmanship.

I had had some doubts about the true nature of the Ghana-Guinea Union. I was struck by the reported differences in the temperament and personality of Nkrumah and Touré, as well

177

as by their obvious differences in language and style. I failed to see how two such strong-willed individuals who liked to be at the head of things were going to surrender enough of the sovereignty of their respective nations to make such a partnership. Of course, this sovereignty could be surrendered on a piece of paper, but I did not see Sékou Touré playing second fiddle in any aggregation led by Kwame Nkrumah. Certain public displays of displeasure during the December 1960 meeting in Conakry caused further misgivings as to the future of the now three-nation Union. I do not wish to give the impression that Touré entered the Union in the first place with an ulterior motive, that of securing a loan from Nkrumah; for I had come to know that Touré had genuine Pan-African interests, and felt him to be sincere in believing that no nation in Africa could be really free as long as any African nation remained under colonial rule.

I found it less difficult to understand Modibo Keita's desire to enter this Union, which included his respected and trusted friend Sékou Touré. The friendship between Touré and Keita made it possible to conceive of a union or federation involving their two nations alone. A federation had been attempted by Mali—then Sudan—and Senegal in 1959, but this federation, known as the Mali Federation, had been dissolved because of dissension between the leaders. Senegal seceded from the Mali Federation on August 20, 1960, and under the brilliant leadership of Léopold Sédar Senghor had become the independent Republic of Senegal. Modibo Keita and his followers had then proclaimed their nation the independent Republic of Mali on September 22, 1960. Despite his first un-

fortunate experience, Modibo Keita was journeying to the
Republic of Guinea three months later in the hope of gaining
strength, support, and stature for his nation by joining the
Ghana-Guinea Union.

I went out to the airport with my diplomatic corps colleagues on December 22, 1960, to greet Prime Minister
Nkrumah and President Keita. After a forty-five minute wait,
during which we sought refuge from the broiling sun in the
waiting room, we were summoned outside to line up in the
places previously designated by the Protocol Chief. Within a
few moments a Soviet IL-18 plane came into view, landed on
the airstrip, and taxied toward the tarmac.

President Touré arrived as the plane came to a stop, and
moved forward to greet Nkrumah as the latter, dressed in a
business suit, swagger stick in hand, descended from the plane.
The two leaders greeted each other warmly, and the band
played their national anthems. Touré and Nkrumah reviewed
the Guinean troops and then walked over to greet the diplomatic corps. After introductions the two leaders disappeared
inside the airport waiting room.

We had hardly time to order a cool drink at the airport bar
before being told that President Keita's plane was about to
land. Again we lined up on the tarmac for a repetition of ceremonies. Out of the sky came a small DC-3, piloted by an Air
France pilot (Nkrumah's IL-18 was piloted by Czechoslovakians, as were the planes acquired later by Guinea). A very tall
man, wearing a flowing white *boubou,* white hat, and white
sandals, open at the heels, stepped from the plane. I realized
that this was President Keita of the Republic of Mali, but he

179

looked more like an African king stepping out of the pages of a history book. As I watched President Touré greet the Malian leader, I was glad that I was not going to play opposite him in a basketball game.

We had been informed that the three leaders would meet from December 22 to December 25. A reception had been planned for December 23 and a dinner the following evening. Then, without any explanation, we were told that there had been a change in plans and a stag-buffet dinner at the Présidence on December 23 was to be followed by a reception the same night to which all diplomats and their wives were invited.

My curiosity was piqued by this change of plans, but I did not go out of my way to seek an explanation. I noticed at the stag dinner, however, that President Touré, Prime Minister Nkrumah, and President Keita were seated at the same table, but there was no interpreter present to enable Touré and Nkrumah to converse. This struck me as slightly odd, but I would not have given the matter a second thought if my wife had not asked me why there was no interpreter with Touré and Nkrumah throughout the reception. There were long intervals during the dancing on the terrace when Touré and Nkrumah had the opportunity for discussing the problems confronting their Union, but they didn't seem to be making any effort to talk. Once my wife had asked her question, I began to observe these two men closely. It was obvious that Touré was not his usual congenial, charming self. By contrast, Nkrumah was smiling at the guests and giving the appearance of enjoying every moment of the festivities.

180

By mere chance, I stumbled on one possible explanation of Touré's visible discontent. Apparently, Nkrumah was insisting that he had to return to Accra to spend Christmas. Touré could not understand this sudden desire to change plans which had been agreed upon months before. Nkrumah's excuse might have been believed by the Americans, but it didn't stand up well in a Muslim country. As I speculated about other reasons for Nkrumah's sudden departure, I remembered that he had been trying to get Guinea to pay the interest on the $28 million loan in foreign exchange rather than in Guinean francs. He had not succeeded in getting Guinea to consent to paying in anything other than Guinean francs. Perhaps this was Nkrumah's way of showing his pique.

Whatever differences might have existed between Touré and Nkrumah during this meeting were not revealed in any way by statements made by either leader. At the conclusion of the meetings, it was pointed out that the decision to form the Ghana-Guinea-Mali Union had been reached to facilitate the co-ordination and promotion of a common economic and financial policy. Two special committees were to be formed to consider ways and means of achieving these objectives. An agreement had been reached to co-ordinate the diplomatic activities of the three states and to hold four yearly meetings respectively at Accra, Bamako, Conakry, and Accra. Regrets were expressed over the "inadequacies" and "failures" of the United Nations to settle the crisis in the Congo. It was announced that the three leaders intended to withdraw their troops from the Congo as an expression of their dissatisfaction with the UN policy. Certain African chiefs of state were soundly reprimanded for "compromising" African unity and for "reinforcing neocolonialism."

Nkrumah and Keita departed as they had arrived, with appropriate airport ceremonies and farewells. Their visit and the resulting Ghana-Guinea-Mali Union represented, perhaps, another victory for Nkrumah in his persistent search for a Pan-African Union. Only history would show whether there had been any real value or lasting quality to this three-nation pact.

I did not see these three leaders together again until the following month, when they gathered in Conakry to journey together to the meeting of what was then known as the Casablanca Group. It may be recalled that their delayed arrival in Casablanca caused the press to speculate that they had stopped over in Guinea to formulate a stop-Nasser strategy. Gamal Abdel Nasser, the United Arab Republic leader, who was also attending the meeting in Casablanca, was said to desire recognition not only as leader of the Arab world but also of Africa. It is possible that these leaders discussed details of the Casablanca meeting, but they did not delay their departure from Conakry for this reason. It was simply a question of a fuel shortage—temporary, but long enough to throw off the departure schedule.

As usual, I was on hand for the airport ceremonies at the request of the Protocol Chief. Nkrumah arrived in his sleek Soviet IL-18 with its Czechoslovakian pilots, and then Keita came in from Mali in his DC-3. The wailing of police sirens announced the arrival of President Touré at the airport, so the Protocol Chief asked us to line up again—this time for the departure ceremonies. Liberian Ambassador S. Edward Peal led the way in the absence of the dean of the corps, the Bulgarian Ambassador. Ten minutes later we were still standing in line and there were no signs of activity in the waiting room. After still another ten minutes, I asked Ambassador Peal to suggest to the Protocol Chief that we could wait in more comfort inside. As Ambassador Peal approached the Guinean official, the soldiers on the tarmac came suddenly to attention. We thought the leaders were at last coming out to the planes. Incidentally, I should have mentioned that President Touré also had an IL-18 at his disposal as a result of a flight connecting Guinea with Prague. Thus there were two IL-18's at the airport to transport the three leaders and their huge delegations to Casablanca.

Instead of coming out to the tarmac, Touré, Nkrumah, and Keita turned and disappeared through the front entrance of the airport building. In a moment the sound of motorcycles and automobiles could be distinctly heard, and in a few seconds it was possible to see, beyond the corner of the building, a procession moving in the direction of Conakry.

For the first and only time during my stay in Guinea I saw a look of embarrassment on the face of Protocol Chief Sassone. He announced quietly that there would be a delay of an undetermined duration. He promised to notify us when to return to the airfield. He had hardly finished speaking before the Ghanaian IL-18 took off, after a brief warm-up, in the direction of Sierra Leone.

Not until later that day when we finally assembled at the airport to see Touré, Nkrumah, Keita, and some of their

183

Ministers take off in Nkrumah's IL-18 was it possible to piece together an explanation of the strange events of the morning. It had been discovered too late that fuel was going to be needed not only for Touré's IL-18 but also for Nkrumah's. Ordinarily no problem would have been created by this demand, for there seemed to be ample storage tanks in and around the port in Conakry. However, the Ministry of Commerce, responsible for importing fuel from the Soviet Union, was in the middle of negotiations with Western companies owning storage tanks in Guinea to force these companies to store Soviet fuel in their tanks. The latest Soviet shipment had yet to be stored, consequently no kerosene, the fuel used by IL-18's, had been brought to the airfield.

To complicate matters, the nearest tanks containing kerosene were in Sierra Leone, in the sterling zone. Guinea was no longer in the franc zone, and complete arrangements had yet to be made for foreign exchange in areas such as Sierra Leone. Foreign exchange presented no problem to Nkrumah, nor did the sterling zone, for that matter. Nkrumah, therefore, sent his plane to Sierra Leone for refueling and had it return to Conakry to pick up the leaders and their aides for the trip to Casablanca. The others were to follow as soon as the Guinean plane could be fueled. Everybody sighed with relief when Nkrumah's IL-18 soared into the Guinean skies en route to Casablanca.

The visit of the Soviet Union President of the Presidium is the only other visit by a foreign dignitary that merits mention here. Surprisingly enough, the Sukarno visit that preceded Brezhnev's by several months was relatively unimportant and prosaic and gave one the impression that Sukarno was either bored, tired, or both, and was merely going through the motions. I do not recall anything outstanding that was said or done during Sukarno's visit. As for Brezhnev, it was already rumored in Guinea that he was the man to watch as a possible successor to Khrushchev. Nobody was prophesying or betting, however, that Khrushchev was going to be pushed out of the Soviet picture so unceremoniously, and that Brezhnev would become the First Secretary of the Soviet Communist Party by 1965.

Two events outside the borders of Guinea set the atmosphere for the visit of the representative of the Soviet Union. The first was the disclosure of the assassination of Lumumba in the Congo. The second was the announcement that the IL-18 bearing Brezhnev to Guinea had been harassed by French fighter planes in the air over North Africa. French sources alleged that the Soviet plane had failed to give advance notice that it would be entering North African airlanes, and when it was challenged had failed to give proper identification. The death of Touré's friend and the harassment of his distinguished visitor's plane gave rise to protestations over Lumumba's "untimely" death and the action of the French fighter pilots.

The Guinean Government issued to the press a statement characterizing the harassment of the Soviet plane as proof of permanent hostility on the part of the French Government toward any policy of co-operation and peaceful coexistence. The attack by the fighter planes—that is, their buzzing of

185

the IL-18—was called an act of ingratitude against the very country that had rescued France from Hitler's grip.

I looked to Sékou Touré to make some kind of public statement in view of the importance attached to the Brezhnev visit, but I did not anticipate the exact nature of the remarks he eventually made. I listened carefully to his welcoming address and tried to get the import of what became the much-discussed Touré statement concerning the identical nature of the views of the Guinean Government and the Soviet Government. Touré complimented the Soviet Union for supporting all people seeking independence and for giving tangible aid to the Algerian struggle for liberation. He decried what he described as the treachery of the United Nations, and then declared:

> We have chosen between the forces of exploitation and oppression characterized by imperialism, colonialism, and neo-colonialism on the one hand, and the socialist forces. We do not fear this choice, by the very reason of its obligatory nature, which is imposed upon all people from the moment they become conscious of the conditions of realizing perfectly their own destiny. . . .

Touré added, much as an afterthought:

> If we have translated with courage the sentiments of the Guinean people in affirming that they are not Communists and that the *Parti Démocratique de Guinée* is not Communist . . . , that the state of Guinea is not an organic extension of any people or the clique of any military or financial coalition, nevertheless, we have the firm conviction to be equally the interpreter of the political and moral thinking of our

186

people, by proclaiming the historic thought which is theirs and which is translated by the merciless struggle against all phenomena pertaining to imperialism and colonialism, for the most popular democratization of our society and for the installation of structures which emanate exclusively from the interdependent interest of the people of Guinea and other peoples of the world.

Touré finally spoke the passage which became discussed in many capitals of the world:

> Yes, the international policy of your Government [USSR], which we have observed, is deeply engaged in this route of peaceful coexistence, without any ideological or other conditions. Let me be allowed to affirm, therefore, in this respect, the identity of the views of the Government of Guinea with the people and the Soviet Government.

This was the furthest I had ever heard Touré go in expressing the Guinean position vis-à-vis the Soviet Union. At that moment I had the impression that the Guinean policy of positive neutrality was moving closer in the direction of neutrality in favor of the East—something which I had predicted since July 1959 unless the West matched words with deeds. There was certainly nothing in the joint statement issued at the close of the Brezhnev visit to dispel my impression. It was not until the expulsion of the Soviet Ambassador in December 1961 for alleged meddling in the internal affairs of Guinea and of its Youth Organization, that the pendulum swung back toward more neutral positive neutrality—if such is possible.

This joint statement referred to above highly praised peaceful coexistence, and condemned the imperialist aggression against the Republic of Congo fostered under the flag of the United Nations. It declared legitimate the Government of Antoine Gizenga in the Congo, and decried the "atrocious slaughter" of the great patriot Lumumba. It lashed out at the colonialist war in Algeria. It indicated that agreement had been reached on Soviet-Guinean co-operation in economic, scientific, and technical fields. It stated that Soviet assurance had been given for an increase in the delivery of machine equipment, petroleum products, and consumer goods, and for the purchase of traditional Guinean exports.

I saw a highly pleased, smiling, and confident Soviet representative climb into his IL-18 after putting on a great show of affection and friendship for an equally smiling President Sékou Touré. I did not foresee—and I don't believe Brezhnev did either—that within less than a year the Soviet Union's troubleshooter, Anastas I. Mikoyan, would be journeying to Guinea to attempt to salvage Guinean-Soviet relations left in the air by the precipitous departure of Soviet Ambassador Solod.

X

Soviet Shortsightedness

Often as I walked beside the ocean in the evening during 1961, I could not help but wonder about the speed with which Russia and its satellites had moved into Guinea in 1958. Walt Rostow had pointed out in 1960 that there had been a distinct shift in Communist policy toward Asia, the Middle East, and Africa at the close of the Korean War. Rostow had maintained that the new Communist policy was based upon the concept that the Soviet Union could make use of the aspirations of the peoples and the governments of Asia, the Middle East, and Africa without resorting to force. Here I was in Guinea seeing this very thing come to pass and observing the validity of Rostow's idea that the Communist policy in developing countries since 1953 had been based upon the exacerbation of any possible points of friction between the developing countries and Western powers. The Soviet Union as well as the other Communist bloc countries had entered Guinea through the open door of economic aid and technical assistance, and by so doing had built up an image of willingness to aid an emerging nation, in contrast to Western reluctance to lift a hand.

I was reminded of the unsuccessful attempt on the part of the Soviet Ambassador in December of 1959 to mar the obviously good effects of the Touré visit to the United States by publishing a report that the United States had endangered the life of the President of Guinea by refusing to grant permission to land the IL-18, on which Touré was being brought from Eastern Europe to North Africa, on the last leg of his series of state visits. Supposedly the IL-18 had developed some kind of difficulty and had requested permission to land at the U.S. military air base in Libya. I was confronted with this report at a reception at the Présidence by an obviously agitated official from the Guinean Ministry of Foreign Affairs. I listened carefully to his statement and reassured him that I would report to him as soon as I had all the facts in hand. I told the Guinean official that I felt positive that no American would do anything that might endanger the life of President Touré. I sensed that here was the hand of Soviet Ambassador Solod, attempting to create sufficient friction between the United States and Guinea to nullify the warmth generated by the successful Touré trip to the United States. I did not give my Soviet counterpart the satisfaction of seeing me leave the Présidence right after my conversation with the Guinean official. Instead of going to the residence in Donka after the reception, I went to the chancery to prepare a query concerning the Libyan matter.

I received a reply two days later. I decided not to dignify this ploy of Ambassador Solod's by going to the Guinean Foreign Ministry with my reply. I decided instead to wait until that evening and deliver my reply at the reception at the

Présidence in honor of the safe return of President Touré from his month-and-a-half visit to foreign capitals. At the Présidence I waited until I was standing in a group that included Minister N'Famara Keita, Minister Fodéba Keita, Acting Foreign Minister Louis-Lansana Béavogui, and a Foreign Ministry official. After exchanging greetings and a few bantering remarks, I announced that I wanted to give my answer to the report which I had received two days ago concerning the alleged American involvement in endangering President Touré's life. I said that in the first place the report was an unmitigated falsehood, put out by somebody who wished to disturb the cordial Guinea-U.S. relations, or else by somebody who would be much better off incarcerated in a Siberian work camp. The Guinean Ministers grinned at this observation.

I then asked the Foreign Ministry official whether the person who had told him the story had told him also that there were two airfields in Libya and that the IL-18, if it really wanted to land, had only to notify the airfield where passenger planes entering Libya always landed. The official admitted that he had not been told anything about the existence of an airfield for passenger planes in Libya and seemed somewhat confused. I asked him if it didn't strike him as somewhat odd that the pilot of the IL-18 had approached a military airfield under the pretext that he needed to land and had made no effort whatsoever to communicate with or to land in the airfield regularly used by planes such as the IL-18. I then turned and pointed to President Touré, who was circling among the guests in the crowded reception room, and said that he certainly looked hale and hearty to me, and to the best of my

191

knowledge the plane had carried him to his destination in Morocco, and from thence to Guinea, without mishap. I concluded that this whole matter of endangering President Touré's life must have been the figment of the imagination of someone suffering from African sunstroke. Everybody in the group, including the Foreign Ministry official, laughed heartily. I shook hands with each one and then left the group to engage President Touré in conversation concerning his recent trip.

President Touré made no allusion to any incident over Libya, and I, of course, made no mention of the nature of my conversation with his officials. The President thanked me very warmly for the reception which had been given him in the United States and expressed his appreciation for the sincere manner in which Americans had made the Guinean delegation and himself welcome.

As I assessed the situation after the reception, I decided that my Soviet counterpart had received no mileage from his sabotage effort. Just before leaving the Présidence that evening, I had gone up to the Soviet Ambassador and said that I hoped the pilots and the plane that had brought President Touré to Conakry had made a safe return trip. I was smiling as I spoke to Solod, and he returned the smile and said the return trip had been without a mishap.

Speaking of Ambassador Solod reminds me of another incident during the visit to Guinea made by Patrice Lumumba in August 1960, when President Touré decided to take Lumumba for a ride in his open Cadillac through the streets of Guinea and indicated that the members of the diplomatic corps as well as the Guinean Ministers should come along. Rather than attempt to have each ambassador ride in his own car in the procession, it was decided that the Guinean Ministers and members of the diplomatic corps would follow the President's car in a bus.

Under ordinary circumstances, this would have been a sensible way to take care of a last-minute decision to transport members of the diplomatic corps. The only problem was that the bus to be used had been made in Czechoslovakia. To ride on such a bus in Czechoslovakia would probably be a delightful pleasure, but it was something of an ordeal in a tropical climate. The windows on this particular bus could open only a slight bit at the top, and since the bus was not air-conditioned, it was literally hot as Hades when filled with passengers. Nevertheless, when the Protocol Chief gave the word, I entered the bus by the side door and sat next to the Minister of Justice, Damatang Camara. Other Ministers and several members of the diplomatic corps were distributed throughout the bus, but I noticed that Ambassador Solod was not aboard. At that moment I looked out the window of the bus, which was parked in the huge yard of the Présidence near the automobiles of the various diplomats, and I saw Ambassador Solod and his chauffeur trying to make their way unobtrusively to the Ambassador's car.

What I did next cannot be found in any protocol book for diplomats; but then protocol was something that was sometimes honored in the breach in Guinea, where the political as well as the physical climate of the country was always hot. Obviously, Ambassador Solod had decided that he was not going to suffer with the rest of us; he was going to make the trip in his car with the windows rolled down all the way. I stepped to the door of the bus, called to my Soviet counterpart, and told him to come on over and join the rest of the proletariat in that air-conditioned Czech bus. For a moment there was silence, then the Ministers and the diplomatic corps members roared with laughter. Solod turned red, grinned sheepishly, and walked over to the bus. I rose and bowed as he entered the door, and as I sat down again the Protocol Chief gave the signal for the bus to follow the President's car.

Perhaps I should have explained that prior to this bus incident I had come to know Solod fairly well, that is as well as an American could get to know a Russian in a place like Guinea. It so happened that Solod liked to swim. He liked to hunt too, for that matter, but my contact with him was in connection with swimming. For some reason, which my neighbor, Ambassador Schroeder, and I never figured out, Solod began coming from Conakry out to Donka during the lunch period to swim in the ocean just off the stretch of sand adjoining the American and West German properties. He showed up the first time when I was just coming out of the ocean after a brief dip before lunch. I looked down the beach and saw two men approaching, one slightly in front of the other, and both in swimming trunks. I could not believe my eyes, for the men drawing near at a fairly swift walking pace were Ambassador Solod and his chauffeur. I approached to speak to the Ambassador, and his chauffeur came to attention. If you have never seen a man in swim trunks, with rather large feet, come to attention in the sand, you cannot fully appreciate this scene. This was rather strange conduct for a chauffeur, I thought. The man was in all likelihood a soldier and Solod's bodyguard.

Solod asked me if it was all right for him to swim, and inquired about the water. I told him the water was pleasant and I hoped he'd enjoy himself; an occasional shark was supposed to grace these waters, but none had as yet been polite enough to greet me, and I trusted that he would be as fortunate.

Solod brought along his bodyguard twice after his first visit. He then began to come alone. He did not show up every day, but when he appeared, Ambassador Schroeder and I would swim out a little distance with him and discuss the weather, the temperature of the water, the Guinean coastline, Guinean climate, university education, the prospective visit of President Brezhnev. Solod had a sense of humor and appreciated light banter. We never discussed communism, capitalism, the cold war, or the political situation in Guinea. Ambassador Schroeder and I knew that Solod's presence there was unusual, because on the public beach in Conakry the Russians always remained in a group, and there were certain individuals who appeared to be keeping the group under surveillance.

Toward the end of December 1960, a newspaper article, originating in Lisbon, expressed the conjecture that the Russians were engaged in building a submarine base near the Los Islands just across the way from Conakry. I probed into this matter, although I cannot outline here what I did to find out whether the rumor had foundation.

195

Several days after the publication of this article, however, and after its discussion in diplomatic circles, Ambassador Solod appeared on the little beach at Donka accompanied by three very attractive women. I did not know whether his guests were members of his Embassy staff or whether they were the wives of his staff members. I had gone into the water shortly after noon, and was coming out for lunch before returning to the chancery. I met Solod as I was entering the residence gate. Looking at him and at his three guests, I asked him quietly if these were his new submarine tenders. Solod looked at me quizzically, laughed, and then ran down to dive into the ocean. Neither he nor I ever made another allusion to the subject of submarines. I should add, however, that the Russians were not building a submarine base off the Los Islands between 1959 and 1961. Of this I am certain.

I noticed toward the end of January that Ambassador Solod was becoming increasingly preoccupied and less jovial than he usually attempted to appear. I concluded that he was getting on edge as the time drew near for the visit of Presidium President Brezhnev. On the night that President Touré held a reception at the Présidence in honor of Brezhnev and the other members of the Russian delegation, I called aside my colleague Hugh Jones, the British chargé d'affaires and told him that I intended to play a little joke on Solod. I didn't tell Hugh Jones what I intended to do, but merely asked him to stand by. In a few moments Solod approached with President Brezhnev and introduced us. Solod gave our names, titles, and the countries we represented. I could not help but notice that there was a world of difference in appearance, manner, and dress between Nikita Khrushchev and Leonid Brezhnev. Brezhnev was solidly built, but not fat. He would have made a good wrestler or fullback. He looked like a businessman and was dressed very smartly in a dark blue suit, black shoes, white shirt, and blue tie, with his white handkerchief showing at the proper length. Brezhnev spoke no French, but he had an excellent French-speaking interpreter.

We talked in generalities for a moment, and then I told Ambassador Solod that I had a question to ask his visitor. I turned to President Brezhnev and with a perfectly straight face told him that his representative, Ambassador Solod, was doing such an excellent job in Guinea that I wondered whether or not there was any chance that he might ever be sent to the United States or to the United Nations. I said that I thought it would be a wonderful experience for him, and it would be a pity if he did not get the opportunity to see my country. As soon as Solod realized what I was saying, he began to get very red in the face and looked somewhat anxiously in the direction of his visiting dignitary to see how he was reacting. Was Solod wondering whether Brezhnev would think that he had prompted me to do this to help him get out of Guinea, the heat and humidity of which bothered him greatly? Was he hoping that Brezhnev was going to realize that I was talking with my tongue in my cheek, and that he would not take the suggestion seriously? At any rate, that sheepish grin, which I had seen once before during the Lumumba visit, appeared on Solod's face as he awaited Brezhnev's answer. The latter merely said that he had no jurisdiction over the placing of diplomats, as this was handled in another bureau. He asked me how I liked my tour of duty in Guinea, and after my reply excused himself to continue on to meet other members of the corps.

Neither Solod nor I ever referred to my suggestion to Brezhnev, even though he returned to the beach at Donka after Brezhnev's departure, accompanied by his wife, who had come to Guinea on the same plane that brought the Brezhnev delegation. Solod's wife found the Guinean climate very difficult, and she only visited the post periodically. A pleasant, middle-aged woman, she spoke neither French nor English, and depended on her husband to interpret for her.

I used to ask myself why it was that despite the Soviet $35 million line of credit and the friendly side of Solod's personality revealed to the Guineans, the Russians were making such slow progress in Guinea. There were times when the Czechoslovakians appeared to be the fair-haired boys because they had rushed in the "small arms" in the early days of Guinean independence. I used to wonder also why it was, if the odds in Guinea were so great against the West, and the West was doing so little to overcome these odds, that the Communist bloc countries did not succeed in taking over Guinea during this transition period.

It was true that although Sékou Touré was a Marxist in orientation, he was not a Communist and he had no desire to see his country taken over by the Russians or the Chinese. For that matter, he didn't want to see Guinea taken over by the Americans, French, British, or Germans. Despite Touré's wishes, however, Guinea's flirtation with the Communist bloc countries, made possible by the treatment received by this republic after it had legally achieved its independence, carried Guinea almost to the brink. That Guinea did not become a satellite may be attributed partly to luck, partly to Touré's maneuvers, and partly to mistakes made by representatives of the bloc countries. There were certainly no specific actions taken by the Western powers in the crucial days of Guinean independence that may be pointed to as having prevented Guinea from becoming a Communist satellite. Neither can it be said that the West deliberately did not act because it wanted Guinea to have a bitter experience with the bloc countries. Let it not be forgotten that the Russians have not lost out as yet in India, and they seem to have worked out a *mariage de convenance* with Nasser's United Arab Republic.

Today it is my considered judgment that if the Russians had not had such confidence in the Master Plan for Africa, and such disdain for Guinean intelligence and Guinean administrative ability, they might have succeeded in scoring an overwhelming success and securing Guinea as a bridgehead for further African conquests. The Russians made the mistake of looking down their noses at the Guinean people, and began trying too hard to drive a bargain too quickly. They were not alone in this, for other bloc representatives erred similarly. But the Russians became impatient and imperious, and they exposed their hand in Guinea just as they did in the Congo during the early days of the crisis there.

The Russians, as did representatives from other bloc countries, came to Guinea, a country with widespread unemployment, and did not hire a single Guinean to work in their chancery or in their residences. The Guineans, a friendly people by nature, could not understand this and interpreted it as distrust. Furthermore, Russians and other bloc technicians, as for example Czechoslovakians, became involved in advising Guineans in the various Ministries and in aid projects. These technicians were not always tactful, and they did not seem to sense the importance of African dignity. They became too dogmatic, too exacting, and too unsympathetic. At the same time the supplies and equipment sent to Guinea by the Communist countries were not coming up to Guinean expectations. The stories of inferior consumer goods foisted on the people were only too true. The real strain in Soviet-Guinean relations became apparent with the hasty departure of Ambassador Solod in December 1961, after the Government decided that his Embassy was involved in aiding Russian-trained or Russian-motivated Guineans to take over the Youth Organizations and infiltrate the Guinean Democratic Party and the Government.

There is, of course, more to it than what I have outlined above. It appears to me that the Eastern European Communist countries forgot to include Communist China in their Master Plan for Africa. When Khrushchev was praising the Communist Chinese in a speech given in 1955 for "throwing off the yoke of foreign oppression," he little dreamed that these same Communist friends were going to become in 1960 and 1961 his chief competitors in Guinea, as well as other parts of Africa. Incidentally, the Communist Chinese had operated in Guinea at a disadvantage. They made the mistake of sending as their first Ambassador a man who could not speak French, and he was accompanied by a woman inter-

preter in a predominantly Muslim country. With the arrival
of French-speaking staff members, and the later offer of a $25
million interest-free loan, the Communist Chinese were in
business. Instead of leasing villas for their personnel, the
Communist Chinese bought up a number of desirable ones
along the ocean front in Donka. They were the first to set up
a trade fair in Conakry, and this fair drew great throngs from
all over Guinea. (The United States would not even consider
setting up a trade fair in Guinea.)

I learned that from time to time Chinese technicians would
arrive in Guinea by plane, spend a day or so at the Hôtel de
France in Conakry, and then disappear into the interior to
begin the work of teaching Guinean farmers how to increase
rice production. Some of the farmers looked upon these new-
comers as possible threats to their livelihood, and the Guinean
Government had to see to it that the Chinese Communists did
not arrive in too great numbers.

Daily I passed a small store, not far from the center of Conakry, which the Embassy of the People's Republic of China
kept well stocked with literature—in French—that praised the
"operation boot-strap" which had brought victory to the
Chinese. The Guineans were assured in this literature that a
similar victory could be won by the Guinean people if they
were willing to sacrifice and to follow closely the example of
their nonwhite friends, the Chinese. The Chinese were not
reluctant to let the Guineans know that their experience
offered more authentic hope for the Republic of Guinea than
the experience of white people anywhere in the world.

The efforts of the Chinese Communists in Guinea were

aided and abetted by the arrival of Nguyen Thong, a French-educated scholar, who was sent as Ambassador by North Vietnam. The few staff members of the Embassy of the Democratic Republic of Vietnam were very aggressive. Their versatile information officer obligingly kept Radio Guinea well supplied with anti-American propaganda, the use of which sent me charging into the office of the Minister of Foreign Affairs with a stiff oral protest.

Observers on the scene in Guinea long before there was open discussion in international circles about a Sino-Soviet dispute could see that the Russians and the Chinese Communists were in competition and set on going their separate ways. Some highly placed admirers of the Chinese Communists among the Guinean Ministers did not hesitate to point out to me the significant parallel between the Guinean and the Chinese experiences. Numerous were the trips made by Guinean delegations not only to Moscow, but also to Peiping.

The longer I stayed in Guinea the more I became convinced that we should think in terms of a Chinese Communist-Russian Communist confrontation rather than in terms of an East-West confrontation. There were, of course, the daily confrontations of Western and Eastern diplomats in the local struggle for the minds and the attention of Guinean officials. There were similar confrontations in the efforts to gain insight into the objectives of the Touré Government. But rather than a confrontation, the basic policy of Western powers in Guinea at this period seemingly consisted of uncoordinated, half-hearted "foot-in-the-door" operations. On the other hand, the Chinese and the Russians went all out in Guinea with the realization that success in this new republic might open doors elsewhere in Africa.

What puzzled me somewhat was that some Guineans who spoke admiringly of the Communist Chinese did not seem to be bothered by the ruthless suppression of the individual and the shocking cost in human beings which had marked the ascendancy of communism in China. The same observation could be made of those who felt that certain phases of the Soviet experience might prove helpful in Guinea. These Guineans were more interested in the much-talked-about material accomplishments of the Chinese, in an amazingly short time, which had elicited praise even from Khrushchev. After all, the highly organized Guinean Democratic Party was geared to keep the people on their toes, and it wanted quick results. If it were a calculated risk that *investissement humain* might turn out to be something other than voluntary labor, the risk still had to be taken for the sake of rapid progress.

It is my belief that the Russians made a serious reappraisal of their economic and technical assistance programs in Guinea. This was particularly in order with the placing of Ambassador Solod over the bureau dealing with the Levant and sub-Saharan Africa. This question of reappraisal was true for the other Communist bloc countries still operating in Guinea. They realized that their efforts had not been marked with overwhelming success, despite their sponsorship of scholarship and aid programs, their sending and receiving of delegations, their attempts to move into Guinea on all fronts —diplomatic, nondiplomatic, economic, social, and cultural. They were forced, as were the Western powers, to reconsider the Guinean foreign policy, which had as its cornerstone "positive neutrality." For a long time the West considered this policy to be a façade that covered up distinct leanings toward the East. The East also considered it to be a façade that concealed an affinity for the East. Guinea's overt disenchantment with the Soviet Union merely strengthened the belief that more effective techniques and approaches had to be found to cope with the Guinean situation as well as with situations in other emerging African nations.

Numerous African students, including some Guineans attending institutions in Communist bloc countries, have attempted to return home or have requested permission to change to Western educational institutions because they encountered racial discrimination in the Soviet Union and other Eastern European countries. Students from Ghana and Nigeria involved in racial incidents which resulted in injury to some students, as well as the death of one, have been particularly vigorous in protesting specifically against racial discrimination in the Soviet Union. Some African students with whom I have discussed this problem have appeared to be thoroughly disillusioned as a result of their experiences in Eastern Europe.

The Republic of Guinea has served as a laboratory as well as a meeting place for the West and the East. This republic, born much as an infant that has had its umbilical cord so rudely and unskillfully severed that healing from ordinary medication has been unsuccessful, has shown the world how difficult it is for a developing country, even within the United Nations, to maintain its sovereignty. It has shown the bitter experiences which threaten a nation beset with economic, political, cultural, and social problems. Although nominal independence was achieved in 1958, there is no question that the struggle is still going on in Guinea to make this independence a reality.

XI

Visiting Americans

I am sure that on more than one occasion American Embassy officers have lamented the fact that so many high-ranking Washington officials or members of Congress have descended upon the various capitals around the world to investigate this or find out about that. These officers probably felt that their time could have been spent in much more profitable and constructive ways.

In Guinea, however, I welcomed and looked forward to visits by American officials and members of Congress, because I felt that they needed to come to Guinea to get a first-hand view of the situation. They could not get a true picture from Washington briefings—conducted often by desk officers who had never been in Guinea—or from stories in daily papers and periodicals—stories written in some instances by those who had been denied entrance into Guinea. Although my post was a long distance from Washington and not easily reached, I did receive many visitors, official and unofficial, who made it their business to come to this African republic to see for themselves. In one instance I was host to forty newspaper editors and reporters who came from all over the United States—May Craig, who used to cover the Washington scene and ask Presidents her inimitable questions, came along to ask me a few. On another occasion, thirty internes of an AID (Agency of International Development) program sponsored by Boston University spent two days traveling in Guinea. Not too long after this, Bernard Blankenheimer, a very able official from the U.S. Department of Commerce, and several American businessmen made a significant visit to Guinea. No visitors to Guinea did more to strengthen anemic American-Guinea rapport than Senator Stuart Symington (Dem.) of Missouri and former Governor Averell Harriman of New York (Harriman had not yet been appointed to the various posts he held under the Kennedy and Johnson administrations).

Before proceeding further, let me point out that our problems in Guinea would have been utterly impossible to solve had I not had the support and co-operation of members of our Embassy staff such as Deputy Chief of Mission Anthony Ross, John Cunningham, Philip Heller, Roger Bearce, Wayne Kirchwem and Wilbur Petty (USIS), Howard Williams, Genevieve Rowan, and Robert Adams.

Senator Symington decided to include Guinea in his African itinerary of December 1959. I was not concerned whether the Senator's reported presidential aspirations motivated his African tour. The important thing was that he intended to come to Guinea. He was the first high-ranking American to visit this new African republic, and he arrived fortuitously in December, shortly after President Touré's return from his highly successful series of state visits. The Senator was accompanied by Attorney Fowler Hamilton, who became Director of the Agency of International Development for a period during the Kennedy administration.

I was happy that the American Senator and his colleague were so well received by the people of Guinea. President Touré and his Ministers were very pleased that an American Senator, and a potential candidate for the Presidency, had seen fit to visit their country. Senator Symington and I called on President Touré, and with my help as interpreter the two men had a lengthy and profitable conversation. The Senator met and talked with the leading members of the Government during his three-day stay. He asked us very keen and penetrating questions during the Embassy briefings and gave evidence of a remarkable grasp of the situation in Guinea.

Although the Senator was favorably impressed with the work being done by our one English-language teacher, he let me know that he was concerned that only one teacher had been sent in answer to a request from President Touré himself. Senator Symington was dismayed to discover that terms had yet to be worked out by the International Co-operation Administration (ICA) which would enable some 150 Guinean students to come to the United States to study under the terms of the October 1959 cultural agreement signed in Washington.

Senator Symington was very much impressed by the fact that wherever we went in the official car with the American and the Ambassadorial flags flying, Guineans, old and young, stopped to wave, call out friendly greetings, and applaud. The Senator told me that this was the first time he had ever seen this happen. I do believe that he must have concluded after three days of this kind of treatment that the showing of friendship was genuine and not something arranged for his visit.

I saw the press reports of a news conference given by the Senator upon his return to the United States from his fifteen-day tour of eight African countries. His five suggestions for strengthening the U.S. position and counteracting Communist influence in Africa interested me greatly. He proposed:

> 1) One billion dollars in American aid each year; 2) Fewer restrictions on the use of our aid funds; 3) Increased exchange of American and African students, teachers, and others to spur education in Africa; 4) Expansion of American diplomatic and assistance missions in Africa; 5) Increased training in African languages for Americans sent to work in Africa. (*St. Louis Post-Dispatch*, Jan. 31, 1960)

The Senator expressed the opinion that in most of the free countries of Africa the Communist position was either equal or nearly as good as the American position, but he admitted that in a few African countries the Communist position was better. He called for better medical care, better education, and a higher standard of living for Africans.

In his report to the U.S. Senate on his African trip, the Senator related the extremely favorable observations and impressions he had heard President Touré express concerning his 1959 visit to the United States. He inserted in the *Congressional Record* a message of thanks which Touré had

210

asked him to deliver to the American people, and then said
the following:

> Mr. President, during my recent trip to Africa, I had the
> great honor of meeting with leaders of some of the newly inde-
> pendent, developing nations of that continent. None was more
> impressive than President Sékou Touré of the Republic of
> Guinea.
>
> President Touré knows and understands the problems which
> an emerging nation must face. He has the determination and
> foresight, which I am sure, meet the challenge of the future in
> a manner that will benefit his nation and the world.
>
> President Touré made a lasting impression on those who
> met him during his recent tours of this country. This trip was
> an example of what can be done between nations if there is
> a mutual exchange of ideas and plans.
>
> I hope that there will be many more such visits and ex-
> changes between our peoples and those of African nations. . . .
> (*Congressional Record—Senate*, Feb. 1, 1960, p. 1512)

Fortunately for us, Senator Symington's interest in Guinea
did not end with his return to America. It is my understanding that he began to question the government agencies about
why so little assistance was being given to Guinea. He cited
for example one English teacher sent to a country with a
population of two and one-half million people. When he
discovered that the 150 cultural scholarships could not be
granted unless the Guinean Government signed the standard
ICA bilateral agreement, he questioned the validity of a
stipulation which penalized innocent students.

I remain convinced that the unflagging interest and the
good services of Senator Symington had much to do with the
securing of those thirteen American teachers who came to

Guinea to conduct the English-language program during the summer of 1960, and with the enabling of forty-two Guinean students to come to America for study in October 1960. What I have always regretted is that more Americans like Senator Symington did not come to Guinea between 1959 and 1961.

Fortunately for the United States, the presidential candidate, Senator John F. Kennedy, had arranged to send Governor Averell Harriman to Africa on a fact-finding mission in August 1960. Guinean officials did not conceal from me their pleasure at the fact that Harriman was including their country in his tour. Although the Governor came as a private citizen, he was greeted with the pomp and ceremony accorded official visitors. The Guinean Government wanted Harriman to occupy one of President Touré's guest houses, but he decided to stay at the Hôtel de France. As already indicated, the official residence which we were occupying had no facilities for visiting dignitaries.

At the Governor's insistence, I was present at his meetings with the Guinean Ministers as well as at his meeting with President Touré and his Cabinet. I made it a point, however, to see to it that Governor Harriman had the opportunity to speak privately with President Touré at the buffet dinner given in his honor at the Présidence. It was during this dinner, apparently, that Touré told his visitor that I was one of the most trusted and respected members of the diplomatic corps in Guinea.

The high point in the Harriman visit came during the meeting involving Touré, his Cabinet, Harriman, and myself.

We had assembled in the Cabinet Room upstairs in the Présidence. The meeting started on a humorous note. The Governor had prefaced his remarks by telling the Guineans that he and I were good friends but we had one major difference in that we belonged to different political parties. Upon hearing this remark, I half rose from my seat and with a perfectly straight face offered to leave the room so that the Governor would feel free to talk to Touré. President Touré, his Cabinet members, Governor Harriman, and I joined the hearty laughter that met this gesture, which had been understood by all those present.

I was proud to be on the scene that day to witness Harriman in action. He was at all times direct and to the point and could be very blunt when the occasion warranted. He made no apologies for those things for which America stood. He spoke the language easily understood and appreciated by Touré, who responded in kind and also revealed what was on his mind. There was no room for misunderstanding during that meeting. We caught a glimpse of Harriman as he might have been during his ambassadorship to the Soviet Union. All of us were pleased with the meeting of minds.

I had the opportunity to talk with Governor Harriman for four hours during a combination breakfast-lunch at the residence the day before he left Guinea. We explored the problems confronting the United States not only in Guinea but also in Africa in general. I stressed my belief that America could make a real contribution in Africa in the areas of health, education, and social welfare. Before leaving the residence, Governor Harriman graciously presented me with his book, *Peace with Russia,* on the flyleaf of which he had written:

> For John Morrow: With admiration for the fine job you are doing and many thanks for your warm hospitality.
> Averell Harriman, Aug. 1960.

There was no question in my mind that the visit of this man as a private citizen on a fact-finding mission for Kennedy did much to improve and strengthen American-Guinean understanding. No propaganda pamphlets or television broadcasts could have done as much as Harriman had accomplished in his face-to-face confrontation with Touré. Harriman did not share the fear expressed in some quarters that Touré and his Government had gone over the brink. I received the distinct impression that he understood that Touré was an African nationalist struggling to make his nation stable and viable.

It is my firm belief that the report made to presidential candidate Kennedy by Harriman on his findings in Africa had much to do with the "new-look-for-the-better" in African affairs at the State Department immediately after the Kennedy administration came to power in January 1961. It may be recalled that the first important appointment made by Kennedy as President was that of G. Mennen Williams to the post of Assistant Secretary of State for African Affairs. This appointment was important, not because Williams knew anything about African affairs, for nobody knew better than the Africans that the new Assistant Secretary of State knew very little about their affairs. Williams' appointment was important because the President of the United States had seen fit to place a man of his stature in such a post. It implied that Williams had the ear of the President and once he could get his feet on the ground in the African arena much-needed changes could be expected in U.S.-African policies.

Unfortunately, subsequent events did not bear out completely these early hopes about the significance of Williams' appointment. Returning to the question of the influence of the Harriman report, I do believe that his recommendations very specifically effected a change in U.S. policy toward Guinea after April 1961, when the Kennedy appointee to Guinea, Ambassador William Attwood, reported to the Republic of Guinea. I was very happy for my successor, Ambassador Attwood, that there was at the beginning this intelligent appraisal of the Guinean situation and a recognition of the need to cast aside outmoded procedures, techniques, and policies for dealing with African nations.

The reception received by a group of distinguished Americans that came to Guinea in the latter part of December 1960 differed sharply from that received by either Senator Symington or Governor Harriman. The delegation was made up of Senator Frank Church (Dem., Idaho), Senator Gale W. McGhee (Dem., Wyo.), Senator Frank E. Moss (Dem., Utah), and Edward Kennedy, younger brother of the President-elect. Young Kennedy had joined the Senators and their party for the last leg of their African fact-finding tour.

I have often asked myself why it was that this last group

215

of American dignitaries to visit Guinea during my tour of duty received such a cool reception. I think the answer is to be found in the events occurring just prior to their arrival. If it had been within my power to suggest a date for the visit, I certainly would have put it off until a more propitious moment.

I had been made well aware that President Touré and his Ministers were very much irked by the role the United States delegation to the United Nations had played in seating in the UN General Assembly the Congolese delegation sponsored by President Kasavubu. The Guinean delegation at the United Nations had given all-out support to the rival Congolese delegation sponsored by their friend, Patrice Lumumba, who had insisted that he and not Kasavubu was the legal head of the Central Government of the Democratic Republic of Congo. I was aware also that Touré was very unhappy about the treatment received by a message which he had sent directly to President Eisenhower, taking issue with Eisenhower over U.S. support for the UN policy in the strife-torn Congolese Republic. Touré's implied charges that the United States was allied with those nations opposing freedom for the Congo and for other African states had drawn a strong reply from President Eisenhower, which was carried on the front pages of American newspapers on November 26, 1960. In this public reply, President Eisenhower had declared emphatically that the United States had been in the forefront of those nations favoring the emancipation of all peoples. Eisenhower asserted that the United States had warmly welcomed the creation of an independent Congo, and had upheld the unity and territorial integrity of the Congolese Republic through the United Nations, and not by means of unilateral intervention in Congolese internal affairs.

Touré had sent a message to President-elect Kennedy also, but had received a rebuff on this score when Kennedy let him know that he too was supporting the stand taken by President Eisenhower on the role played by the United Nations in the Congo. It seems that Kennedy's reply surprised and nettled Touré, who had expected a difference of opinion between Eisenhower and Kennedy. Touré reacted by carrying out his December 1960 threat to recall Guinean troops from the Congo, made during the formation of the Ghana-Guinea-Mali Union, and cabled the UN Security Council that he was withdrawing four hundred troops stationed in the Congo because of violations of the UN Charter by the UN force in the Congo.

When the American Senators and Edward Kennedy reached Guinea, President Touré had not returned from an official visit to Sierra Leone. I had arranged, however, for my visitors to see Touré on the following Monday morning, prior to their departure from Guinea. In the meantime, the word reached Conakry that an attempt had been made in Sierra Leone to sabotage the helicopter—a gift from the Soviet Union—in which Touré was traveling. It was reported that dirt had been placed in the oil line of the helicopter, and it had been necessary to fly a second plane to Sierra Leone to return the presidential party to Conakry. I did not expect that this incident, if true, was going to put Sékou Touré in a congenial mood for meeting Monday morning guests.

217

It should not be difficult to imagine what happened when we arrived at the Présidence on that morning. The first thing I noticed was that the guards did not come forward to greet me with their usual alacrity. I summoned a guard and asked him to notify the Cabinet Chief that my guests and I had arrived for our meeting with President Touré and his Cabinet. I presumed that the guard delivered the message, for he went into the office of the Cabinet Chief. When he did not return with a reply, and the Cabinet Chief did not appear, I thought this somewhat strange. As the minutes ticked by and no one appeared, I told the delegation members that I had begun to suspect that the delay had some diplomatic implication. I had never waited to get into President Touré's office before, whether I came with visitors or alone. My remarks brought the observation from one of the more candid members of the delegation that they had waited a very long while in Addis Ababa before getting in to see Emperor Haile Selassie.

Prodded by the thought that we had not kept the Guinean delegation waiting at any of the appointments at the White House or at the State Department in the fall of 1959, and by my determination not to have the Addis Ababa wait repeated in Conakry, I stepped into the hall and called a guard. I told him to inform the Cabinet Chief that I had found it impossible to wait any longer, and was therefore returning to the Embassy with my guests. The guard turned in a flash and sprinted up the stairs to the Cabinet Chief's office. Before I could re-enter the waiting room to suggest to Senator Church, the delegation leader, that we should leave, the guard returned to say that the President wished to see us. As I climbed the stairs to the Cabinet Room, I was not sanguine about our chances for a successful exchange of views.

Upon entering the Cabinet Room, in which the Ministers had already taken seats around the long table, I noticed immediately that President Touré appeared tired and was not his usual cordial self. I was conscious also of the absence of banter usually exchanged among the young Ministers. There was something unusually solemn about this premeeting atmosphere.

Scarcely had I finished introducing the Senators and young Kennedy before Touré launched into a lengthy discussion of Guinean history and geography. He skirted the vital problems, which he and I knew from past experience American officials wished to discuss. I suddenly realized that Touré knew that the delegation was supposed to go directly from the Présidence to the airport to depart for Dakar, their last stop. I decided that he was deliberately using up time to avoid an extended question-answer period.

When the Senators and Kennedy did get the opportunity to ask questions, the answers given were not very relevant. It became obvious that Touré was not going out of his way to impress these visitors favorably. I could see the implications for the future if the American delegation left with the feeling that it had been impossible to get first-hand information on troublesome problems which threatened American-Guinean relations.

On February 12, 1961, there appeared in the United States a Senate document reporting on the African tour made by the U.S. Senators. A portion of this report devoted exclusively to Guinea clearly precluded any possible implementation of the bilateral agreement which the Minister of Plan, N'Famara Keita, and I had signed on September 30, 1960, in Conakry. I cannot say that I was surprised by this report, but I was sorry that the conclusions had been reached after only one meeting with Touré, held under none too favorable circumstances. The report said in part:

> There are indications that the performance of the bloc in Guinea has not measured up to its expansive promises. We see no reason for the United States to undertake to obscure this development, or to assist any Communist effort to make Guinea an example of what bloc aid can accomplish. There are limits to our resources and too many African countries which need our help, and which respect our motives. Another issue causing us to advocate a wait-and-see approach is the recent dispatch of large quantities of military supplies from the bloc. The implausible explanation Guinea offers regarding its needs for such arms, including anti-aircraft guns, concerns the purported discovery of arms caches in connection with a "plot" against its borders.
>
> Pending clearer evidence that Guinea indeed wants our friendship and wishes to—and can—preserve its independence from the bloc, we believe that the United States should maintain no more than a token aid program just to keep the door open.

There, spelled out in black and white for the first time, was the very policy which the United States had been following in Guinea since 1959. Nobody had been willing to admit this to me before, even though I had sought through various means to discover what policy had been set for this country where the American Embassy staff had tried unceasingly to establish mutual understanding. In my estimation, it would have been much fairer had I been told this very frankly in Washington before departing for Guinea. If it had not been possible to determine the guidelines before my departure, at least I should have been told the day, the hour, the minute the United States decided its policy. It is a matter of record that we lived in hope, we never despaired, we never stopped fighting for what we thought should be done to assist this developing country in its struggle through a desperate and frustrating transition period.

The report made by the American delegation came as a result of its contact, treatment, and observations in Guinea. I hold Touré himself responsible for some of the conclusions drawn. I think that he was most unpolitical and shortsighted not to have made an honest effort to answer the queries put to him by Church and his colleagues. He had everything to gain and nothing to lose. The press had already printed all kinds of unfavorable things about Guinea—some true and some untrue. He did not have to worry about the exposure of skeletons in the closet. He had only to slug it out as he had done with Averell Harriman, and the Senators might have been impressed by his forthrightness, whether or not they agreed with him. Instead, angry at U.S. policy in the United Nations, provoked by Eisenhower's and Kennedy's replies to his allegations, morose over the alleged sabotage attempt in Sierra Leone, this young African leader stepped to the plate in the U.S. Senate's World Series. He did not go down swinging; he was out on called strikes.

Senator Church saw fit to insert in the *Congressional Record* (Appendix, Jan. 30, 1961, p. A555) very complimentary remarks concerning my ability as a diplomat and representative of the United States abroad. But Senator Stuart Symington had done the same thing upon his return to America (*Congressional Record—Senate,* Feb. 1, 1960, p. 1512). My real concern was the knowledge, after reading the Church report, that tangible progress toward meeting the problems of human suffering abounding in Guinea was not going to be made during the time I would be there.

Deputy Undersecretary of State Loy Henderson came to Guinea in the course of an October 1960 inspection tour of American Embassies and Consulates in sub-Saharan Africa. Although Henderson's visit involved American business, strictly speaking, I saw to it that he got to converse with Minister Abdourahmane Diallo, Acting President in the absence of Touré. My good friend C. Vaughn Ferguson served as the interpreter during Henderson's conversation with Diallo.

It is to the everlasting credit of Loy Henderson that he did his best to secure for me the kind of administrative support which I requested. But not even Henderson could overcome overnight the dearth of trained, knowledgeable Foreign Service personnel in hardship posts in Africa or Asia.

We accompanied this twenty-one-man party of American officials to the airport on October 26, 1960. The guards waved us through customs with a smile and a sharp salute. The passports had already been delivered to the departing visitors, so we walked out to the waiting MATS plane. I asked the young Embassy officer once again if he had checked to see that the passports were in order, and he answered in the affirmative. I stayed aboard the plane a moment to wish the delegation a safe trip to Sierra Leone and a safe return to America. The plane took off and was soon out of sight.

An agitated and displeased commandant of the airport met me at the door of the waiting room. In excited tones he explained that the Americans had left Guinea without filling out exit visas and declarations of foreign currency. I told him that this had been handled by the Guinean Foreign Ministry, and I had been assured that all was in order for a smooth departure. I asked him to check with the Ministry, but he insisted that the Ministry did not run the airfield. He said he intended to instruct the tower to recall the plane. I assured him that he was making a grave mistake, especially since his Government had welcomed these distinguished visitors and had given assurance that all was in order for their departure from Guinea. I suggested again that he would do well to phone the Ministry. The commandant turned and walked toward the tower.

Our conversation lasted almost twenty minutes, and I hoped that the plane was out of the range of the tower's signal by that time. Within five minutes, however, the commandant came strutting back to announce that the tower had radioed the plane and the pilot had agreed to return. I told the commandant that not a single American was going to get off that plane and set foot on Guinean soil; that if he had anything he wanted signed it would have to be taken to the plane. I told him that anybody who got on or off that plane would have to climb over me.

Twenty minutes later the plane landed. I went aboard and asked Loy Henderson why the plane had returned, particularly since the Guinean Foreign Ministry had handled the passports. He said the decision to return was made after a brief conference aboard. It was felt that future American-Guinean relations would be better if the letter of the law were obeyed.

Meanwhile, two guards had brought the necessary visa and currency cards to the door of the plane; these cards were filled out, stamped, and returned to the commandant's office. For the second time that day I bade the visitors farewell, only this time I asked them not to return, even if they heard that I was a prisoner at the airport. Everybody aboard laughed. The plane took off.

I returned to the Embassy to prepare one of the stiffest notes that would be sent during my tour in Guinea. This note brought back the quickest response of any ever exchanged in Guinea. The Guinean note graciously apologized for the unfortunate incident created only through misunderstanding on the part of certain functionaries in the Ministry and at the airport. It reiterated the pleasure on the part of the Guinean Government to have welcomed the distinguished American visitors.

Several days later I received a personal letter from Loy Henderson with the dateline Monrovia, Liberia. He said in part:

Dear John:

It was a pleasure to see you during my two visits to Conakry. Please don't feel concerned about our early return visit. It did us no harm and it may be that the Government of Guinea will be conscious of our desire meticulously to respect its regulations. . . .

While on the subject of visiting Americans, I must not overlook the two visits made to Guinea by vessels from the U.S. South Atlantic Fleet on amity patrol. The first was made by two destroyers under the command of Commander R. A. Foreman. The ships spent three days at the harbor in Conakry toward the end of December 1960, and afforded many Guineans their first glimpse of an American naval vessel.

I accompanied Commander Foreman and two of his officers on protocol visits to the President of the National Assembly, Saïfoulaye Diallo, and Defense Minister Fodéba Keita. Guinean Ministers visited the Commander's flagship, and enlisted personnel and officers from the ships visited Conakry, played basketball with the Guineans, and purchased souvenirs. Commander Foreman invited Embassy officers and our wives aboard the U.S.S. *Vogelgesang* for dinner, and I reciprocated by having a party the following night at the residence, to which were invited the ships' officers and the staff members of the British and West German Embassies. The three-day visit went off without incident, and the spirits of the members of the Western embassies were lifted by the enthusiasm and good nature of the visiting Americans.

The second visit by ships of the U.S. South Atlantic Fleet came about as the direct result of events in the Congo. Through coincidence, the same Guinean troops transported

to the Congo in August 1960, in U.S. C-130's under the flag
of the United Nations, were returned home in February
1961 on U.S. vessels called upon in this emergency by the
United Nations. These troops, recalled by Sékou Touré in
December 1960, had been waiting in the Congo for transportation. It fell to the lot of Rear Admiral Allan L. Reed, an
outstanding naval officer, to cancel scheduled amity visits in
order to bring the Guinean troops to Conakry. The LSD's
under Reed's command reached Conakry a day or so after
the departure of Leonid Brezhnev of the Soviet Union, and
welcome signs and plastic Soviet flags were still on display
in the main streets of Conakry.

The official landing ceremonies got under way after Admiral Reed, his aide, and I called on President Touré, and
President Touré and his Ministers returned the call. In
reality, President Touré came down to the port, but only his
Ministers went aboard the flagship *Hermitage* to return the
call. As a shore cannon began firing, the first contingent of
Guinean troops marched ashore, smiling at the plaudits and
shouts of relatives and other onlookers. It was to be several
hours before the troops and gear could be unloaded, and
President Touré and his Ministers left after the landing of
the first contingent of troops. On all sides could be heard
stories of friendships struck up among the Guinean soldiers
and the U.S. sailors and marines aboard the vessels on the
way to Guinea. The language barrier had not prevented the
establishment of mutual respect and good fellowship.

Just before the start of the reception which we held at the
residence that night in honor of Admiral Reed and his officers,

I was made an honorary member of the *Hermitage* crew and presented with the ship's emblem. At the conclusion of the reception the Admiral insisted that we should be his guests at dinner at the Hôtel de France. This was to be something of an outing for us and a change from the formal dinners at the residence or elsewhere. We reached Conakry at 9:15 P.M., and upon finishing a leisurely meal Admiral Reed suggested that we have coffee aboard the *Hermitage*. His car led the way to the port. When it turned into the port area, its headlights revealed not only that the large iron doors were shut, but that they were guarded by a squad of soldiers.

I had never seen the gates closed before, day or night. I motioned to one of the guards, who stepped forward, came to attention, and saluted. He seemed reluctant to answer my question about the armed guard and the closed gates. He said finally that the locked gates and the guards had been ordered by the Defense Minister. I stepped out of the car to go over to speak to Admiral Reed, and noticed a crumpled pile of plastic Soviet flags lying under a street light. This sight gave me some inkling of what might have happened. At that moment several sailors and marines returning from shore leave came into sight.

I outlined to Admiral Reed what probably had happened and instructed the guard to call the Defense Minister to let him know that I wished to enter the gates with my guests. I told the Admiral that I felt it advisable to clear all American personnel out of the vicinity. The easiest way to do this was to carry everybody out to the residence in Donka. Reed and his officers agreed to this idea, and in a moment the necessary order was given. There were approximately twenty to twenty-five sailors, marines, and officers in the gathering by that time. The sailors and marines climbed into a navy truck and jeep which had been brought ashore for errands and shore patrol. There were two cars for the officers, and three rode with my wife and me.

Before leaving the port, I told the Guinean guard that we could be reached at the residence. Thereupon I led through the silent streets of Conakry probably one of the strangest midnight processions that ever graced that tropical city. When we reached the gates of the residence in Donka, the two soldiers assigned as guards (around-the-clock guards were supplied by courtesy of the Guinean Government) opened the gates and stood at attention as the curious cortege rolled by. The most startled ones were the cook and his helpers, who were still cleaning up from the reception. The cook told me that a call had come from the Defense Ministry with the information that the Defense Minister would be happy to see us down at the port.

I thought that I would give the Minister, who lived not far up the street from the residence in Donka, sufficient time to reach Conakry. We learned from the assembled naval personnel that the Guinean police had stopped several enlisted men who were carrying plastic Soviet flags found in the streets of Conakry. As far as could be ascertained, nobody had been arrested, but the flags had been taken by the police. When I heard this story, I suggested that only three of us should return to Conakry until the matter was cleared up.

Admiral Reed, his aide, and I went back to the port, supposedly to meet the Defense Minister. Once in the area I saw
the Deputy Defense Minister standing under the light near
one of the gates. He stepped forward briskly and told me that
naval personnel had committed a serious offense. I asked him
about the nature of this offense. Pointing dramatically to the
pile of plastic Soviet flags, he said it was a serious offense to
desecrate the flag of a friendly country in Guinea. He said
that these flags had been pulled down by Americans. I said
that I knew no American would willfully desecrate the flag
of another nation; furthermore, I was told that some of these
flags had been picked up from the street for souvenirs. I
myself had seen flags dangling from poles and lying in the
street that very morning and had remarked to the Embassy
chauffeur that the Department of Public Works usually
cleaned up the flags very quickly after the departure of the
dignitaries.

When I asked the official how many men had been appre-
hended, he admitted that no arrests had been made, but the
flags were collected. He didn't give a satisfactory explanation
about locking the gates or posting a guard. I asked for further
proof that the flags had been taken by the Americans. He said
the proof was in two jeeps locked inside the gate. I said that
I wanted to see this evidence, and the Deputy Minister
ordered the gates opened. I hurried over to Admiral Reed and
suggested that he go aboard the *Hermitage* and wait for his
aide and me.

The aide, the Deputy Minister, and I walked toward the

pier and came upon a Guinean soldier guarding two navy jeeps. The Deputy Minister, without a flashlight, reached under the seat of one of the jeeps and pulled out one Soviet flag. He walked over to the other jeep and pulled out one plastic Soviet flag. I had expected to see the jeeps piled high with flags, and expressed my surprise at seeing only two. I told the Deputy that there was very little to go on but I would like to have the flags for a few hours. This appeared to me to be a case of souvenir hunting which he was mistaking for something else. I reminded him that the Americans had been from one end of Conakry to the other buying souvenirs of their visit to Guinea, and I could easily understand why they might pick up these flags lying around in the street. The Deputy handed me the flags, but said that he would have to have them in the morning.

Before returning to the *Hermitage* I walked over to the Customs Office located near the main gate to phone the all-clear signal to the officers and men in Donka. Out of the darkness from the other side of the Customs Office came the familiar voice of Embassy officer Darold Keane. Keane stepped out of an Embassy car, obviously very glad to see me, and said that he knew I would come to his rescue. When I asked Keane what he was talking about, he said that he had been locked in the port area since leaving one of the ships at 10:30 P.M. He had been told that the only way he could get out was to be released by the American Ambassador. I called a guard and told him to let Keane out of the gate. Keane made some kind of a record going through that exit. I telephoned my wife and returned to the *Hermitage* to await the arrival of the men from Donka. Very shortly everybody was aboard and accounted for.

I told Admiral Reed that as far as I was concerned the incident was closed. This appeared to be an attempt to blow a minor incident into something bigger, but the whole thing had fizzled out. Reed expressed the hope that I would experience no problems because of the events of the evening. I assured him that there would be no repercussions, and bade him good-bye. The ships were to leave early that morning at high tide.

I got back to Donka and found the employees still cleaning up, but this time they were doing so as a result of the big midnight snack served the navy men. The staff had enjoyed the unusual events of the evening and went away contented when they realized they had been paid for overtime.

I had to go out to the airfield the next morning to welcome another group of dignitaries. I handed the Deputy Minister a large envelope after shaking his hand and asking him if he had slept well. He thanked me and went over to join his colleagues. I have always wondered why he never asked me for that second plastic flag.

The only reference ever made to this flag incident came several weeks later when the police arrested some British seamen for gathering plastic flags. Defense Minister Fodéba Keita met me at a reception at the Présidence and said laughingly that he could have had "my Americans" picked up for the same thing. I replied that I was surely glad he had not done so, because it would have meant my walking all the way out to Camp Alpha Yaya with two marines to get them out.

This would have delayed the ships' departure by a few minutes, and rear admirals never liked to be late leaving a port. The conversation ended in laughter.

I had been very happy with both visits of the American ships. Nothing marred that feeling. It was a thrilling experience to be piped aboard those flagships in December 1960 and February 1961, to hear the national anthem and inspect the guards of honor. On each occasion I had experienced that tingling sensation up and down my spine as I stood at attention during the national anthem. Each time I had that taut feeling in my throat and had hoped that there was no telltale evidence of moisture in my eyes.

One curious side effect of the comings and goings of the U.S. C-130's in August and the ships of the U.S. South Atlantic Fleet in December and February was that the Western and Eastern members of the diplomatic corps, as well as the members of the Guinean Government, thought that I had had a hand in planning all of this. In reality, the only thing which I had a part in planning was the good-will visit of the destroyers in December. When I heard about the presence of U.S. ships on amity patrol in waters off the coast of Africa, I felt it would be a wonderful idea if they could stop at Guinea. The Government of Guinea cooperated with the idea. It would have been a losing cause, however, to try to convince anybody in Guinea that I was not behind the idea of bringing in American planes and LSD's. I must admit that I was impressed with the good that they did in promoting a feeling of friendship toward America. We could use all the good will we could get!

XII

American
Shortsightedness

The economic plight of Guinea resulting from its severance of ties with France, the initial emphasis of the Touré Government on the political rather than the economic, and the constant pressure of the Communist bloc countries combined to make Guinea's position on the international scene precarious. The support given by Guinea to the Soviet position at the United Nations had raised questions concerning the credibility of the professed Guinean policy of positive neutralism. Each time I raised this question with Guinean officials, they were quick to point out that the anticolonial posture of the Soviet Union at the United Nations coincided with their objective of independence for all African nations.

In spite of the discrepancies which marked the carrying out of Guinean foreign policy—and there were many—I remained convinced that the cornerstone of this policy was positive neutralism. Touré insisted repeatedly that the Guinean diplomatic doctrine was based essentially upon the interest of the Guinean people; that the Guinean people could not live in isolation from the rest of the world and overcome their eco-

nomic difficulties; and that his nation was seeking the friendship, brotherhood, and co-operation, in economic and cultural spheres, of all governments willing to respect Guinean
sovereignty. Touré proclaimed:

> Guinea is not the extension of any country. Its regime is not
> tied to any regime in the world; its experiment, inscribed in
> the cadre of African realities, has for its concern rehabilitating
> this Africa, and serving, in a dynamic and positive fashion, the
> cause of its independence and its unity. (Speech delivered in
> Conakry on May 1, 1959)

Never at any time during my stay in Guinea did I entertain
the naïve belief that President Touré or his colleagues could
be won over to the West. I did believe that it was possible for
the West to help this African leader to observe more closely
the professed policy of positive neutralism, but I felt that the
West had to accomplish this by deeds and not by words. It
was not a question of pouring millions upon millions of aid
dollars into a country that did not have the trained personnel
for heavy industry. It was rather a matter of showing intent
and willingness to help a developing nation meet its major
problems of development at a critical moment in its history.

Moscow saw to it that the whole world knew that it had
offered Guinea a $35 million line of credit in August of 1959.
What was not so well known was that the stringent terms of
this offer caused the Guinean Government to delay its acceptance until March 1960. There existed also a convention
on technical and economic aid concluded between the Republic of Guinea and the Federal Republic of Germany (March
1959) which provided a number of German experts to aid

234

Guineans in improving methods of handling fish, raising cattle, and processing meats. The West German and Guinean Governments had under consideration a commercial treaty that involved the exchange of West German machines, motor vehicles, consumer goods, and technical equipment for Guinea's iron, bauxite, diamonds, coffee, and bananas. Negotiations were under way for a commercial treaty between the Republic of Guinea and the United Kingdom which became effective in October 1959.

The question asked within as well as outside diplomatic circles in Guinea was whether or not the United States intended to give aid to Guinea. French and Lebanese businessmen attempting to hold on in Guinea made frequent visits to the chancery with their appeals. Wherever I traveled in the country, people still engaged in small businesses besieged me with questions. For some reason these people seemed to think that I could exert some kind of magic influence in Washington that would get my country to aid the sagging Guinean economy. They felt also that I could get President Touré and his Government to lighten those regulations which were forcing foreign enterprises out of business.

I told all of these seekers that my country did have a genuine interest in preserving Guinean independence and stability, but that I had no way of knowing at that time what decisions were going to be made about aid. This was the truth, but I always felt that those asking the questions did not believe me. I said that I could not interfere in the internal affairs of Guinea in the regulation of business enterprises, but I suggested to the French businessmen that they concentrate on getting their country to reach mutually acceptable agreements with the Guinean Government on monetary, political, and cultural matters.

Since my arrival in Guinea the major accomplishments had been the strengthening of mutual understanding and respect between the United States and Guinea, and the supplying of one English teacher. Naturally, I was perplexed by the silence in Washington on the specific, urgent requests and suggestions for an effective aid program which had been sent from our Embassy. I could not understand why apparently no action had been taken on recommendations prepared by the International Co-operation Administration (ICA) long before I had become Ambassador. I had decided finally that there might be some effort to start discussions during the state visit to the United States of President Touré scheduled for October 1959. But September fast drew to a close, and there was little that could be accomplished during an official visit to Washington unless the groundwork had been carefully laid in advance.

I had been scheduled to arrive in Washington several days ahead of the Guinean delegation to make sure that there were no loose ends to mar President Touré's official visit. In the midst of last-minute preparations for the trip, I received word from Washington that an official from the International Co-operation Administration was to arrive in Conakry the next day to begin negotiations with Guinean authorities on the standard bilateral agreement. For more than three and one-half months, despite repeated queries, we had remained in the dark concerning aid for Guinea. Now, four days before my departure date of October 18, word had come of the imminent arrival of an aid official.

I knew the Guineans well enough to realize that they were going to be extremely suspicious about any effort to negotiate an agreement so close to their visit to America. They could easily believe that I had been deliberately deceptive in not letting them know in advance that my country contemplated approaching their Government concerning an aid agreement. I was aware too that the officials with whom we had to deal were probably making their own preparations for the seven-nation tour with President Touré. I thought that the timing of the arrival of the Washington official was extremely bad.

The official arrived the next day, and we spent the morning going over the details of the agreement which I was to present to President Touré that afternoon. I stated very emphatically my objections to the timing and the purpose of his visit. After reading through the statement, which I was seeing for the first time, I warned that the Guineans were not going to be willing to sign it. The official felt that I was unduly pessimistic and said that the favorable atmosphere surrounding the Touré visit to America ensured the success of these negotiations. I replied that President Touré was going to be more interested in learning whether the United States was supplying a plane to transport the Guinean delegation to Washington than in discussing the details of an agreement at this time. I assured the official that nobody wanted to have an effective working agreement with the Guinean Government more than I did, and I pledged to do my utmost to achieve one, despite my misgivings.

The ICA official, my acting deputy, and I met with President Touré at the Présidence that afternoon. After presenting my colleagues, I thanked the President for receiving us at such short notice. I outlined the nature of the proposed bilateral agreement and succeeded in getting Touré to agree to appoint a working party to explore its details. I requested a meeting the next day (Saturday), since my departure was scheduled for Sunday. Touré indicated that the Ministers participating in the meetings would not be available until Monday. He concluded the interview in his usual fashion by saying, *"D'accord en principe,"* which meant simply that he had heard our proposition, and the interview had come to an end.

The ICA official seemed very elated as we left the President's office, and when we reached the chancery he wanted to send word to Washington that Touré had agreed in principle to the terms of the agreement. I told him that I could not sign such a message because it would give Washington the wrong impression. He reminded me that Touré had said *"D'accord en principe."* I said that the Guinean President used this expression frequently in his conversations with his Ministers and with members of the diplomatic corps, and that it was merely a polite acknowledgment that the President had been listening. Touré would not state any opinion on the agreement until it had been examined carefully by his advisers. I also ventured to say that the moment Touré's advisers read the clause pertaining to certain privileges for technicians, they would reject the whole agreement.

It was fortunate that the original message which the ICA

official wanted to send to his agency never left the chancery. The negotiations, started on Monday, October 19, 1959, came abruptly to a halt the following day when the Guinean officials made it clear that their Government would accept no agreement which encroached upon their national sovereignty. They declared that they had granted no special privileges to Russian, Czechoslovakian, or Polish technicians, and they had no intention of extending special privileges to American technicians. The American official was very much upset over the Guinean opposition and greatly disappointed at the failure to secure the acceptance of the standard ICA agreement by the Guinean Government.

When the word came through in Washington about the breakdown in negotiations in Conakry, I was not the least bit surprised. I was called into a hastily arranged meeting with State Department and ICA officials. An ICA man told me that I would have to return to Guinea and educate the Guineans on the ways of doing business with the United States. I asked him to suggest specifically how one educated the officials of a foreign country who charged that the insistence upon special privileges for nondiplomatic personnel encroached on their nation's sovereignty and felt that any pressure tactics constituted an insult to African dignity. The official in question, who up to this point had been quite vociferous and somewhat arrogant in tone and bearing, became silent.

I left that meeting and I left Washington with a feeling of deep frustration and bewilderment at the attitude of some of the officials in the International Co-operation Administration toward Guinea in particular and Africa in general.

239

Among other things I had detected an attitude that seemed to be: Guinea will either sign this agreement or else. I got the impression that these officials did not particularly care whether Guinea received aid or not. There seemed to be a complete unawareness of the ferment on the African scene, and of the fact that all Africa, as well as Asia, was scrutinizing the United States-Guinean relationship to discover whether the United States had placed a new priority on Africa and at last was formulating policies that were "responsive to African realities."

To be perfectly frank about it, during my entire tour of duty in Guinea, I encountered only five ICA men who showed the understanding, technical expertise, and empathy absolutely essential for dealing with the ofttimes sensitive officials of developing nations. I can remember the names of four of these men, Jack Hood Vaughn, Marc Gordon, Bill Freeman, and John Canning. Unfortunately, I cannot recall the name of the fifth, but I do remember that he spoke with a foreign accent and was quite perceptive. Jack Hood Vaughn, who later left ICA—the best thing that he could have done—to go to the Peace Corps (later he became Ambassador to Panama; Assistant Secretary of State for Inter-American Affairs; Director of the Peace Corps), was particularly effective during his visit to Guinea, even though the Guineans did not sign the agreement at that time. It was always my regret that ICA was unwilling to give Vaughn the rank or the authority to exercise his good judgment in the negotiations with the Guineans. With the necessary authorization from Washington—which we could not get—and with Vaughn and myself working as a team, I believe that we could have broken that particular aid impasse many months earlier.

I do not wish to convey the impression that I felt bitter toward the ICA. I was well aware that there were others within its ranks during the period in question who realized how important it was to prove to the emerging African nations the validity of the often expressed U.S. commitment to help them develop economically and politically while maintaining their sovereignty. Unfortunately, these knowledgeable individuals lacked the authority to put their ideas into action. Certainly the attempt to secure American technicians for countries like Guinea was a very ticklish and difficult matter. Those who had the desired skills and a speaking knowledge of French were usually reluctant to leave the United States to serve overseas for a twelve- or twenty-four-month period. Furthermore, the conditions under which they might have to live and work in some areas raised questions about health hazards as well as creature comforts.

I can well understand why the ICA felt obliged to seek the very best possible conditions, including diplomatic immunities, for its personnel. It is a fact, however, that other Americans not under ICA jurisdiction were recruited to work directly for the Guinean Government by the African-American Institute. The vast differences in pay and perquisites created an unfortunate atmosphere among these Americans and others living under better conditions. Those who experienced difficulty in getting promised compensation or housing,

241

or who ran afoul of customs because of an unwillingness to pay unexpected duties were not in the best frame of mind to perform their assigned tasks.

A Guinean official at the Education Ministry summed up the situation by saying that the only people who complained constantly about their working conditions were the Americans. He contrasted their attitude with that of the Russians, Czechoslovakians, and East Germans who supposedly accepted without question the conditions in struggling Guinea. What this official ignored or did not wish to acknowledge was that Soviet, Czechoslovakian, and East German technicians had to carry out the orders that came from above. American technicians were free to stay or leave—several did leave without giving notice.

Fortunately for our standing abroad, the Peace Corps later proved conclusively that Americans could go into any country in the world without deep freezers, rugs, and other outward signs of our modern civilization and perform as effectively as people from any other country. Peace Corps members did much to remove the idea that Americans always clamor for special privileges and complain about the disgracefully low level of foreign culture and civilization. In fact, the excellent volunteer group of students known as Operation Crossroads, sponsored by the Rev. James Robinson of New York and chaperoned in Guinea in the summer of 1960 by the Rev. William Coffin, Yale University Chaplain, really paved the way for the Peace Corps in Africa.

I did wonder at times, however, what agency actually exerted the most influence on the foreign policy of the United

States. It often appeared to me that the ICA, responsible for the outlay of huge sums throughout the world, was making the State Department play second fiddle in the decision-making department. This might not have been true of American dealings eleswhere in the world, but it seemed to be the case at least as long as I was in Guinea.

Whatever may be said to the contrary, the Guinean Government remained unwilling to sign the standard ICA agreement in the form originally presented in the fall of 1959. The document, finally signed by the Minister of Plan, N'Famara Keita, and myself in Conakry on September 30, 1960, was the outgrowth of prolonged and frustrating negotiations in Washington as well as in Conakry. The signing ceremony was witnessed by Guinean reporters and one French reporter and photographer. A release concerning the agreement appeared in the *Agence Guinéene de Presse*, but no publicity was given it in America until an enterprising reporter of *The New York Times*, Dana Adams Schmidt, got wind of it a month or so later. As a result of his prodding, spokesmen for the State Department and for the ICA admitted that a bilateral agreement had been signed. I never did understand this reluctance to admit that the agreement had finally been concluded.

This bilateral agreement was considered a very significant event by members of the diplomatic corps in Guinea, who had come to believe that the United States and Guinea would never reach a meeting of minds. It was considered so significant by the Soviet Union that it called Ambassador Solod home two days later. When the Soviet Ambassador returned to Guinea, it was announced that Soviet engineers were to arrive soon to begin work on the railroad connecting Conakry and Kankan. The Soviet authorities did not know what I had reason to believe, that the agreement between Guinea and the United States would not be implemented during the remaining months of my tour of duty in Guinea. And it was not!

I had hoped that the United States was going to assist in the construction of the Konkouré Dam, not because I wanted Touré to have a prestige project, but because I felt—as had the French—that such a dam was necessary for the further development of industry in Guinea. I felt that Touré was as good a risk as Kwame Nkrumah any day, and was much more forthright. Nkrumah received American aid for his Volta Dam project. Any hope that Touré might have had concerning the possibility of American support for the construction of a dam on the Konkouré River to provide electric power for an aluminum smelter—a project already seriously considered by the French—was not realized. It was well known that Touré favored this project very much because he felt that the electric power not used by the smelter could be utilized by the towns and villages of Guinea. The Soviet Union expressed a willingness to aid in the construction of this dam, but nothing appeared to come of this offer while I was still in Guinea. It was always my feeling, however, that the Soviet Union was going to build a dam for Touré sooner or later, just as it agreed to build one for Nasser.

I was frequently asked by visitors to Guinea—official as well as unofficial—what was wrong with relations between the United States and Guinea. I could have answered this question merely by stating that it was inevitably a long-drawn-out process to establish good relations between two such different nations. This would have been dodging the issue. It was closer to the truth when I replied that Africa had not been on the U.S. priority list until fairly recently. I felt that the awareness in U.S. governmental circles of the situation developing in Africa had come as much from developments in the United Nations as from reports from African capitals—reports which were all too frequently ignored or acted upon too late. In the United Nations there had been a marked increase during 1960 and 1961 in the number of African nations that had become member states. The articulate delegates from Africa insisted that the powerful nations belonging to the United Nations support rather than thwart the role of the UN in aiding "Africa's revolution achieve success in as peaceful and just a manner as possible." The United States was finding it increasingly difficult to secure the support of African and Asian nations for UN measures in which it was particularly interested. But nobody seemed to be connecting developments at the United Nations with United States policy in Africa.

In the 1959 report, "United States Foreign Policy," prepared under his guidance, Dr. Melville J. Herskovits of Northwestern University pointed up the initial handicap facing the United States in Guinea: the United States did not have even a consular agent in Conakry when Guinea became independent in 1959; furthermore, the United States took more than a month to recognize the Touré Government, which had gained independence according to legal procedures established by the French Government. Calling attention to the "extreme caution" exercised by the United States in granting aid to Guinea, the Herskovits report declared:

> The United States has never had a positive, dynamic policy for Africa. Until very recently, we have looked to continuing control by friendly European powers as a guarantee of stability and dependable co-operation and have been reluctant to acknowledge the principle of self-government as fully applicable to its people.

The American position in Guinea between 1959 and 1961 was not helped by the uncertainty and "extreme caution" that slowed down the decision-making processes. In my estimation, the reluctance to take the necessary measures to establish an aid program in Guinea was partly the result of an unwillingness of Washington officials to endorse the concept that foreign aid is a "normal instrument of American foreign policy." This reluctance did not keep Senator Fulbright from advocating that U.S. foreign policy should move in the direction of making our aid efforts more effective. It should be recalled that Senator Fulbright himself, in his August 1964 attempt to show that reductions in the proposed foreign aid bill would undermine the program as an instrument of foreign policy, remarked:

> In the context of the cold war, the objective of our aid program is not to help build stable and viable nations which will be profusely grateful to the United States, never annoy or displease us and follow us loyally on all international questions. If these were our objectives, a more effective program would be training and equipment of mass armies of occupation.
> Ingratitude is disagreeable but not dangerous, and slavish

compliance is a characteristic for which a free society has no use, either in itself or in its associates.

It's a small consolation to know that the Guinean situation dramatically illustrated the need which the U.S. State Department had for more people with a special knowledge of Africa, and the need for having decisions concerning Africa reached within the higher levels of the Department. Moves in this direction were started during the Eisenhower administration, and radical changes were made in the Kennedy and Johnson administrations. Conclusive proof that the United States had learned a lesson with Guinea was seen in the speed with which it recognized other newly emerging African nations and sent out delegations of high-level Americans to the independence celebrations of these nations. But this is only one facet of a very complicated situation.

Nowhere have I seen the basic problems and the mistakes bedeviling the United States in Africa expressed more clearly, forthrightly, and effectively than in the article, "Lost Goals in Africa" (*Foreign Affairs,* October 1965), by Dr. Arnold Rivkin, member of the Development Advisory Service of the International Bank for Reconstruction and Development. Dr. Rivkin's estimate of the goals lost by the United States in Africa could well be taken as a blueprint that explains the ineffectiveness of the U.S. policy in the Republic of Guinea between 1959 and 1961. Dr. Rivkin is on firm ground when he states:

United States policy in Africa has lost much of its credibility for a large part of the African continent. We have held out hope for more than we have, in the event, been able or willing to deliver. Often the promise of brave words was extravagant and unwise, but what is noticed is that it has not been matched by congruent acts. We have seemed to say one thing and do another.

It is obviously better to make fewer promises and carry them out than to promise and fail to deliver. But I would like to point out also that the inability to make any promises at all or to anticipate favorable action on legitimate requests is just as bad as making too many promises that remain unfulfilled.

In respect to Guinea, Dr. Rivkin is correct in his appraisal of the influence exercised by the European Bureau of the State Department in shaping U.S. policies toward Guinea that caused the relationship between the United States and Guinea to be "severely limited" during a three-year period. Rivkin asserts:

> . . . Policies toward independent African states are also shaped in the European Bureau. The sensitiveness of President de Gaulle, as judged by the European Bureau rather than an independent assessment of the U.S. national interest in French-speaking countries is likely to be a decisive factor. . . . Notwithstanding the existence of the very situation which should have triggered active U.S. interest in Guinea, our respect for French primacy and De Gaulle's wishes prevented our taking action.

Dr. Rivkin reveals that Guinea and Mali, despite a combined population of eight million people, received one-half as much economic assistance as Nigeria with a population of

55.5 million, and Guinea alone received more U.S. aid than Senegal and the Ivory Coast combined. It can thus be seen that Guinean-American relations took a turn for the better during the Kennedy and Johnson administrations even though Rivkin feels that

> In Washington, Africa now has the lowest priority of any area. This has always been more or less State Department practice in making foreign-policy decisions; now it has become a matter of national policy.

One of the reasons my situation in Guinea was often so frustrating was that I became aware of the unwillingness on the part of Washington officials to recognize the fact that Guinea had won independence through a legal and mutually agreed-upon procedure. These officials wanted everyone to exercise great care that nothing was done in Guinea to offend General de Gaulle. It was perfectly clear that De Gaulle hoped that the Guinean experiment would fail and that its failure would serve to deter other French African territories from taking a similar leap toward independence. It was clear also that De Gaulle was motivated in part by personal pique and anger at Sékou Touré because the latter had chosen the occasion of the General's visit to Guinea to enunciate the desires and aspirations of the Guinean people. Nevertheless, American officials were unwilling to heed my fervent pleas concerning the necessity of treating Guinea as an independent nation and making good on our oft-repeated assertions of interest in the self-determination of emerging nations. Instead of seizing the initiative, as urged constantly by the

Embassy in Conakry, and taking obvious and logical steps to enable Guinea to develop constructively, the State Department saw fit to stick to its "notion of residual interest" in its dealings with Guinea. It was impossible to get support even for our proposal that medical teams be sent into Guinea to immunize the people—especially the children—against various diseases and undertake the dissemination of health information. Yet in 1965 this is exactly what was done in Guinea by the good ship *Hope* with its wonderful hospital facilities.

We had the opportunity to prove conclusively to all of Africa that our interest was not limited by our fear for what our NATO allies might think. But we let these opportunities slip by, and the Guineans and others were only too aware that our interest in their welfare seemed to increase only after the departure of the Soviet Ambassador late in 1961, and after the suppression of a second threatened coup in Guinea.

When I think of the care exercised by U.S. officials not to offend the easily ruffled feelings of President de Gaulle in regard to Guinea, and consider the shaky relationship that exists today between the De Gaulle Government and the U.S. Government, I cannot find the words to express my regrets over our missed opportunity. De Gaulle's demands for the withdrawal of American and other Allied military installations as well as of the Supreme Headquarters Allied Powers in Europe from the soil of his country should reveal to all concerned the futility of American efforts to appease De Gaulle between 1959 and 1961.

I am not saying that we should deliberately ignore the views of our allies. I submit, however, that if we lay claim to a foreign policy that endorses the viability, stability, and self-determination of developing nations, we cannot always be in perfect agreement with our allies. I cannot see how we can blow hot and cold in Africa and still expect our policy to have credibility there.

It is not easy to forget the shock and dismay caused by my suggestion that the United States urge France to arrive at a suitable agreement with the Guinean Government over monetary, political, and cultural problems, thus making possible a *détente*. Then there were the reports made by French authorities to the State Department that I was holding France at arm's length, when in reality I was attempting to establish rapport with members of the Guinean Government and gain their respect and confidence. Not to be overlooked were the attempts on the part of French diplomats to sabotage the state visit made by Sékou Touré to the United States in the fall of 1959. Had I not personally fought off these efforts in Paris (en route to the United States in October 1959), in Washington, at the Department of State, and at the White House, there is no telling what effect the French efforts might have had upon the Touré visit. The De Gaulle Government was angry even at this ceremonial show of interest in the Touré Government and wished to diminish—if not cut off completely—the "red-carpet" treatment extended traditionally to a visiting head of state. I shall always believe that the deciding factor in warding off the negative influence the French attempted to exert on the Touré visit was the invitation extended to me prior to Touré's arrival to brief the White House staff on the situation in Guinea. I did not pull any

251

punches on this occasion, just as I had not in my appearance before the Secretary of State and his top advisers. At least nothing happened to mar the Touré visit.

As I have said elsewhere, Guinean Ambassador Telli Diallo, with whom I had established a firm friendship, took me to task during one of his visits to Guinea for having stopped off in Paris in 1959 to consult with the French. I vehemently denied this charge, and explained to Ambassador Diallo that my own Government had forbidden me to have any contact with French officials. I had, in fact, been confined to talking exclusively with the U.S. Ambassador in Paris, his staff, and an Episcopal minister and his wife. I don't think that I ever convinced my Guinean counterpart of this; nor could I convince Guinean officials, for that matter, that the United States did not consult the French Government before dealing with the Guinean Government.

Notwithstanding Ambassador Diallo's understandably bitter attitude toward the French Government, this very loyal and earnest Guinean, a most intelligent and astute lawyer and diplomat, always reminded me of a Frenchman in his actions, mannerisms, and ways of thinking and expressing himself. For that matter, this was true also of Ismaël Touré, the Minister of Public Works, and of Fodéba Keita, the Minister of the Interior. There were no Guineans more loyal to President Touré and to the Guinean cause than these men, yet they were certainly Frenchmen under the skin. They had lived in France for many years and had absorbed French culture and civilization. The rupture with France had not eradicated this influence. So it was with a number of other Guinean officials.

At moments when they were engaged in their most heated declarations concerning the injustices and inequities of the French colonial situation, they sounded like, looked like, acted like French. At a moment, for example, when those French who still remained in Guinea were finding it impossible to repatriate their savings, the Guinean Minister of Education was in Paris trying to convince officials that they should still allow French teachers to come to Guinea. At a moment when President Touré was decrying French perfidiousness, a French Commission was en route to Guinea for discussions— fruitless though they might have been.

Coinciding with my impression of the depth of French influence on members of the Guinean Government and the people of Guinea was my belief that an unmistakable unifying factor in Guinea was the French language, which had become the official language by decision of the National Political Bureau. The mere suggestion that one of the dialects be chosen as the official language was sufficient to evoke rumblings that threatened tribal disturbances. The National Political Bureau effected a compromise as far as African languages were concerned by having them taught in the schools to enable prospective government employees to speak directly to all Guineans. English was decreed the second language of Guinea.

I have come to believe that if the French had exercised more tact, common sense, and diplomacy, and less pique, in handling the severance of relations with Guinea, the situation in Guinea would have been vastly different. The skill with which the French had spread their civilization and language was offset by their shortsighted and immature reaction to an inevitable choice made first by the Guineans. A relationship such as exists between France and the Ivory Coast, or between France and Senegal might have been possible had De Gaulle been willing to accept a *fait accompli*.

Until the 1965 break in diplomatic ties between France and Guinea over an alleged assassination plot aimed at President Touré, some progress had been made between these countries in settling monetary matters and improving cultural relations. For example, more teachers of French nationality could be found in Guinean classrooms than were present in Guinea between the difficult years of 1959 to 1961. Moreover, the Federal Republic of Germany and the United Kingdom did not appear to be any less interested in Guinea than before.

The conclusions of Dr. Rivkin cited above concerning economic assistance given by the United States to certain African nations indicate that Guinea eventually did receive greater assistance from the United States. It did not become known, however, until a near break in diplomatic relations between the United States and Guinea in November 1966 that Guinea had received almost $72 million in U.S. aid—mostly in agricultural products—since 1962.

On the surface, it appeared that Guinean-American relations had been improving slowly but surely since 1962. Then suddenly on October 30, 1966, President Touré ordered the house arrest of the newly arrived American Ambassador, Robinson McIlvaine, and one week later announced the expulsion of sixty-two Peace Corps volunteers and their dependents. These precipitous acts decreed by the highly emotional and oversuspicious Touré resulted in the summoning of Ambassador McIlvaine to the Department for consultations. A break in diplomatic ties was only narrowly averted.

This new strain on tenuous Guinean-American relations resulted from retaliative measures taken by Touré after his Foreign Minister, Louis-Lansana Béavogui, and eighteen other Guineans had been forcibly taken off a Pan American plane landed for refueling at Accra, Ghana. The Guinean Foreign Minister and three other members of the Government en route to a conference of the African Organization of Unity (OAU) in Addis Ababa, Ethiopia, and fifteen Guinean students en route to Lagos, Nigeria, to study English were seized by the Ghanaian police during the unscheduled refueling stop.

The Ghanaian Foreign Ministry charged the Guinean Government with holding some one hundred Ghanaians in Guinea against their will and said that the nineteen Guineans would not be released until the Ghanaians were allowed to leave Guinea. The Ghanaian Ministry charged further that Touré was broadcasting and allowing former Prime Minister Nkrumah, to whom he had given asylum in Guinea, to broadcast insulting, humiliating, and subversive propaganda. The Ministry branded the training of Ghanaian guerrillas in Guinea as "warlike actions" on the part of Guinea.

Touré, asserting that his Government would offer free transportation to any Ghanaian who wished to leave Guinea, justified his arrest of the American Ambassador by saying that he held the United States fully responsible for the seizure of Guinean citizens in transit on an American-owned plane. A

Guinean Foreign Ministry official declared that American officials had given the assurance that the Pan American plane bearing the Guineans would not stop at Accra. This had been believed because Pan American planes had been departing from Liberia and flying to Lagos, Nigeria, without stopping at Accra. Guineans had been boarding these planes in Liberia confident of arriving safely at their destination. The fact that this particular plane bearing Guineans had stopped at Accra gave rise to the belief that the Central Intelligence Agency had alerted Ghanaian officials.

A strong protest from the State Department brought about the release of Ambassador McIlvaine in less than twenty-four hours, but did not prevent an unruly mob from breaking furniture and windows at the Ambassador's residence shortly after his release. The State Department denied any responsibility for the Accra incident, but the Guinean Government insisted that the United States should take steps to secure the release of the nineteen "hostages."

It was not until after a three-and-a-half-hour conference at Addis Ababa on November 5 that Lieutenant General Ankrah of Ghana, leader of the coup against the Nkrumah Government, consented to release the nineteen Guineans. Emperor Haile Selassie of Ethiopia and President Gamal Abdel Nasser of the United Arab Republic finally prevailed upon the Ghanaian leaders to take this step, which prevented a split among the thirty-eight nations in the OAU. President William Tubman of Liberia was in on the first hour and a half of the conference with Ankrah.

The United States authorized the American Ambassador to

Ethiopia, Edward M. Korry, to circulate to OAU member states a strongly worded note criticizing Ghana's arrest of Guinean citizens as well as Guinea's arrest of Ambassador McIlvaine and G. Lambert Ronstrom, manager of Pan American World Airways.

A committee from the OAU visited Guinea and reported that no Ghanaians wished to leave Guinea. Such a report was to be expected, for none of Nkrumah's former security police wanted to risk returning to Accra. Furthermore, none of the Ghanaian students shipped to Conakry from the Soviet Union after the fall of Nkrumah felt free to speak their minds for fear of reprisals after the committee's departure.

Affairs in Guinea had seemingly returned to normal when the American Embassy was informed on November 8 that Peace Corps personnel had one week to get out of Guinea. Typically unpredictable was the "warm" but "regretful" send-off given the Peace Corps volunteers by Guinean Government officials, who hastened to assure these Americans that they were "angry" only at the United States and not at the Peace Corps.

It is a pity that Touré allowed his pride and anger to bring him to the point of expelling the one group that had so much to offer his country. It is unfortunate that he countenanced the house arrest of the American Ambassador and thus flagrantly failed to honor the fundamental concept of diplomatic immunity. For these unwise acts Touré must be held accountable. Equally deplorable is the Ghanaian Government's disregard for acceptable international behavior.

As long as Touré harbors former Ghanaian Prime Minister

Nkrumah, an implacable enemy of the United States, there will continue to be misunderstandings between Guinean and American officials. Nkrumah is convinced that the CIA played a role in the overthrow of his government, and he is not going to let Touré forget this. Touré, for his part, is determined to prove to Nkrumah that he is not following the dictates of the United States or any other country.

The State Department could do nothing less than call home Ambassador McIlvaine for consultations, but I am glad that it did not opt for an outright break with Guinea. I hope that the Department can persuade Touré of the desire still prevailing in the United States to aid his country, and yet at the same time let him know in no uncertain fashion that he must honor the obligations and responsibilities of international dealings.

I am still convinced—these unfortunate incidents notwithstanding—that the nations of the West, and in particular the United States, must remain in the vanguard, realistically and sensibly aiding emerging African nations to develop economically, politically, and culturally while maintaining their sovereignty.

XIII

End of a
Mission

I followed the standard procedure observed by all American Ambassadors of submitting my resignation prior to the November 1960 election, so that the new President might be free to select his own diplomatic representatives. I did not receive word from the Department until the first week of February 1961 that the Kennedy administration had decided upon my successor. I was instructed to seek the written consent (*agrément*) of the Guinean Government for the proposed replacement. I was informed at the same time that the new Secretary of State was considering placing me in another position that would make use of my background, experience, and fluency in French. This word from the Department was followed by a letter from President Kennedy expressing appreciation for the service which I had rendered the United States and indicating that my resignation was to be accepted at a date to be determined.

I was very much surprised to learn that the new administration was contemplating my staying on in another capacity. I was committed to go to a new position as chairman of the

French Department of Atlanta University, from which I had been granted a two-year leave of absence, thanks to the understanding and thoughtfulness of the president, Dr. Rufus Clement, and his board of directors. I had agreed to accept the position at Atlanta University just a month before the State Department had approached me in 1959 about going to Guinea. I felt obligated, therefore, to go to this academic post. On the other hand, there was the question of the challenge offered to me by the Kennedy administration. This could mean only that the new administration was taking this means of recognizing the job which I had attempted to do in Guinea.

For three days and three nights, during spare moments, I wrestled with the decision which was to influence so greatly the future course of my life. Finally, on the evening of the third day, I made my decision. I wrote to Dr. Clement explaining why I had decided to remain with the State Department.

The following day I let the Department know that I was interested in remaining and asked the nature of the new assignment under consideration. It was then that I learned that the Department intended to send me to Paris as the United States Permanent Representative to UNESCO. I was very happy at the thought of serving in Paris in such a capacity.

As the time drew near for me to leave Guinea, I hoped more than ever that the change in administration in Washington meant a change of policy toward Guinea and other emerging African nations. As it happened, my successors to the post in Guinea—two of whom were noncareer diplomats and one a career officer—Ambassador William Attwood (former foreign editor, *Look* magazine), Ambassador James Loeb (former newspaper editor), and Ambassador Robinson McIlvaine, were sent into Guinea by the Kennedy and Johnson administrations respectively with firmer and more knowledgeable commitments than I had had. I was glad for their sake and for the sake of the U.S. position in Guinea that this was the case.

With the suddenness and lack of explanation characterizing many official actions, I learned on March 1, 1961, that before reporting to my new post in Paris I was to report to Washington by March 6 to appear before the Senate Committee on Foreign Relations to be confirmed as Alternate Delegate to the U.S. Mission to the United Nations. I was greatly surprised by this new development, but not overwhelmed. Certain basic realities kept me fully aware that I was not living in a dream world. There was, for example, the seemingly impossible task of closing the Ambassador's residence in three days—three days because I was determined not to leave my wife behind to face this task alone; there were the official calls of leavetaking to be made on President Touré, his Ministers, and my diplomatic colleagues; there were innumerable other details to be arranged before I could feel free to depart.

When I saw President Touré at the Présidence, he expressed in the presence of National Assembly President Saïfoulaye Daillo more than merely polite regrets that I was being called from Guinea. He said that he wished to write President Kennedy about the change, and when I demurred, he asked me to consider seriously staying on in Guinea as a private citizen to serve as adviser to his Government. I explained that this would not be fair to my successor and told him that each U.S. President had the right to choose his diplomatic representatives. I thanked President Touré for his sincere expression of confidence and told him that I could not remain in Guinea because I had agreed already to serve my Government in another capacity. When the Guinean Ministers saw me the next night at a reception at the Liberian Embassy, they were equally warm in the expression of their regret at the departure of my family and myself.

I had my last look at Guinea from the window of an Air France plane that left Conakry on Friday, March 3, 1961. As Conakry faded in the distance, my thoughts turned to the summer of 1958 when I had walked the hot and sometimes deserted streets of Paris vainly seeking passage to Algiers. I had not suspected that summer that I was standing on the threshold of a period that would afford a ringside seat to events constituting the raw materials out of which history is made. I thought about the first morning of our arrival in Guinea, of the warm reception at the airport, and of the subsequent events. I wondered seriously about the items which I could place on the credit side of the American-Guinean ledger. Fate had not decreed that I should have at my disposal a $35 million line of credit, as had the Soviet Ambassador. I had not been able to rely upon a $25 million interest-free loan, as could the Chinese Communist Ambassador. I could not lay claim to having supplied small arms for security purposes and to having secured barter trade agreements in moments of crisis, as could the Czechoslovakian Ambassador. My country had not agreed to construct a huge printing establishment in Conakry that could supply much of West Africa, as had East Germany. Nevertheless, I didn't feel as if I were trying to delude myself in concluding that my mission in Guinea could not be written off as a failure for the following reasons: (1) President and Mrs. Touré and a Guinean delegation had toured the United States during a very successful state visit. (2) A cultural agreement had been signed between the United States and the Republic of Guinea. (3) An American Cultural Center had been opened in Conakry. (4) Fourteen Americans had participated in an English-language project in Guinea. (5) Forty-two Guinean students had come to America to study—the first of some 150 selected for study in American colleges and universities. (6) Operation Crossroads, a privately sponsored, summer work program involving American college students had been admitted to Guinea. (7) Eighteen American teachers were working directly for the Guinean Government. (8) An agreement involving agricultural products had been signed. (9) An ICA bilateral agreement had been signed. (10) Guinean officials other than those who had accompanied President Touré on his state visit had visited the United States. (11) WCBS and WABC television crews had filmed programs involving Americans in Guinea for showing in the United States. (12) United States planes flying under the flag of the United Nations had transported Guinean soldiers to the Congo. (13) Ships from the United States South Atlantic Fleet had twice made goodwill visits to Conakry and had been welcomed by the Guinean authorities. (14) Property for a new chancery was secured and plans for remodeling the existing building drawn up and approved. (15) Mutual comprehension and good will maintained through persistent efforts to keep open the channels of communication, even during periods of crisis, had enabled us to develop firm rapport with President Touré, his Government, and the people of Guinea.

As the Air France plane moved toward Dakar, I thought about our numerous trips into the interior of Guinea and our wonderfully reassuring reception by the friendly Guineans out in the brush. I recalled their eagerness to hear about the great land of America, which wanted all people to be free. I remembered that these people in the brush thought that a straight, unencumbered road would lead them to freedom and peace, where they could enjoy the fruits of independence promised by the Guinean political leaders before the September 28, 1958, Constitutional Referendum. I could still visualize the varied landscapes of Guinea—the flat savannahs, table mountains, steep slopes, low-lying, partially swampy coastal area. I could hear the patter of the rain that fell during the six-month rainy period, and see the dust that settled in our eyes, ears, and nostrils as we traveled back roads during the six-month dry period. I could hear the roar of the beautiful Guinean waterfalls and understand why Guinea was referred to as the "watershed" or "water tower" of West Africa. I could see the pineapples, bananas, coffee, and rice being readied for market.

The thunder of airplane engines brought me back to reality

as we landed in Dakar. One hour later we were bound for France, and after a thirteen-hour flight we reached Orly Field in Paris. Our friends at the American Embassy in Paris were excited over my appointment to the American delegation at the United Nations. I could not reveal at this time my appointment to our delegation at UNESCO in Paris.

With some difficulty, the Embassy secured seats for us aboard a New York-bound TWA plane, and we were met that Saturday evening at the International Airport in New York by the genial and efficient administrative officer of the United States United Nations Mission, Fred Schottke.

We decided to stay in New York overnight and proceed to Washington Sunday evening. This was fortunate, because in the middle of the night I had to seek the services of a nearby hospital. An infection which had started in a toe of my right foot cut on a piece of laterite rock during my last swim in Guinea had started to spread up my leg. Miracle drugs speedily removed any threat of danger, but I had to appear at the State Department and at the hearing of the Senate Committee on Foreign Relations with a shoe on my left foot and an African sandal on my right. I explained that I had received the injury in Guinea, but it had come neither from a hammer nor a sickle.

The setting for my second appearance before the Committee was much more informal than the first had been. The hearings were held in a much smaller room, and the Senators were seated on one side of the table with the nominee on the opposite side. Senator Fulbright was presiding. Also present were Senators Bourke B. Hickenlooper (Rep., Iowa), Hubert H. Humphrey (Dem., Minn.), and Stuart Symington (Dem., Mo.).

Appearing before the Committee that same morning were Philip Coombs, who had been nominated for the post of Assistant Secretary of State for Educational and Cultural Affairs, and George F. Kennan, who was being named Ambassador to Yugoslavia. Neither Mr. Coombs, an executive of the Ford Foundation, nor Mr. Kennan, brilliant career diplomat and noted scholar of Soviet affairs, experienced any difficulty with the Committee.

Senator Fulbright called me to the table, greeted me cordially, and informed the Committee that I had appeared before its members earlier in connection with my appointment to Guinea. He said that the Senators might have some questions to ask me. A busy forty minutes ensued. Senator Humphrey, who was particularly interested in the depth of Communist penetration in Guinea, led off in this hearing, which was open to the public. He asked about the steps taken by the Embassy to meet the Communist thrust. I gave direct answers to the questions of the Senator from Minnesota, hoping all the time that nothing I said would be misconstrued by the press or the public. I did not wish to add to the problems of my successor. Senator Symington followed, and instead of asking questions gave his estimate of what I had attempted to do in Guinea on behalf of America. I was gratified by the generous remarks of the Senator from Missouri.

Senator Hickenlooper was the most persistent questioner that morning, probably because of the nature of the answers given to his questions. He seemed interested in developing the theme that the United States should not give aid to developing countries that appeared to deal with Communist nations. He seemed convinced that Guinea was in that category.

I tried to point out tactfully that it was this very failure on the part of Western powers to aid Guinea in the beginning that had made it possible for the Communist bloc nations to become entrenched there. I indicated that the United States was giving very little aid to Guinea at that moment, therefore our discussion was largely theoretical. I said that I thought Touré was a fervent African nationalist with a Marxist orientation, who did not wish to be dominated either by the Russians or the Americans or the French. I asserted that my fear had been that we would not attempt even a "foot-in-the-door" operation and thus make it easier for the bloc nations to establish their bridgehead in West Africa. I concluded by saying that I felt that the United States should definitely develop an effective aid program in Guinea and try to ensure that Guinea would observe a true policy of neutralism.

During the forty-minute session I had not been asked a single question concerning my qualifications to represent the United States at the United Nations. An official explained after the hearing that the Senators were happy to get first-hand information on the Guinean situation and therefore had kept me in the chair longer than usual.

My mission to Guinea came to an end officially when the United States Senate, convening at noon on March 6, 1961, voted its approval of my appointment as Alternate Delegate (with ambassadorial rank) to the U.S. Mission at the United Nations.

Today, more than five years later, when I think back to my tour of duty in Guinea, I cannot help conjecturing about the kind of aid policies the United States might have followed in Guinea and other parts of Africa if David Bell, Director of the Agency for International Development from 1963 to 1966, had been at the helm between 1959 and 1961. Bell was not afraid to admit that this business of trying to aid emerging nations was extremely complicated, and he did not hesitate to acknowledge that there were weaknesses in current U.S. aid policies. At the same time, however, he worked very hard to develop new and sounder policies. When Bell left the Agency, U.S. aid policies were on much firmer ground as a result of his efforts.

U.S. aid policies are being closely scrutinized by the Senate Committee on Foreign Relations and the Congress. The present difficulties in Vietnam have given impetus to the efforts of Senator William Fulbright, Committee chairman, to develop a foreign aid program which, in his words, "will isolate us from the political and possible military implications that attack our present bilateral system of aiding developing countries." Fulbright has called attention repeatedly to what he calls the "unfortunate side effects" of the bilateral arrangements in Vietnam that have caused the United States to be identified with "certain" political regimes in this strife-torn nation.

The situation in Guinea in 1959 was not like the situation in Vietnam today; nevertheless, the presence in postindependence Guinea of the Communist bloc countries in full force, the unexplained arms build-up in this African republic, the failure of France to settle its monetary and political differences with Guinea, and the long-drawn-out aid negotiations between the United States and Guinea did create an unmistakable atmosphere of crisis there.

This atmosphere was heightened by our knowledge that Khrushchev had revealed as early as 1955 (December 30 speech following visits to India, Burma, and Afghanistan) a blueprint for the Soviet approach in Africa. Depicting the Soviet Union as the staunch opponent of colonialism with no history of colonies in Africa, Khrushchev had proposed moving into the breach as a friend bringing economic and technical assistance to the emerging nations, while allaying suspicions by promising easy terms and noninterference. It was to be only a matter of time, of course, for the Guineans to realize the harsh truth that the costly prestige projects such as sports stadia, huge radio transmitters, jet landing strips, tanks and antiaircraft guns, and a Guinean national airline (operating within Guinea and between Prague and Conakry) did not help to stabilize their struggling economy.

It will always be a matter for debate whether any policy other than our blundering one in Guinea really would have served our interests any better. One of the pervading weaknesses of U.S. aid efforts prior to recognition of the Guinean Government had been the tendency to contribute aid with the idea of combating Soviet influence and saving neutralist nations from the Soviet camp. These ofttimes futile attempts to counterbalance Soviet influence obscured the fact that aid

269

was being given also in the hope of creating stable and secure states. The U.S. efforts to exclude Soviet aid or lessen the political effects of such aid served frequently merely to make us more susceptible to "competitive blackmail" by the neutralist or "nonaligned" states.

In Guinea, we were confronted with a leader, Sékou Touré, who declared himself to be a "neutralist" in the same fashion as the leaders of other developing countries of Africa and Asia. Even prior to our confrontation with Touré, neutralists had created difficult problems for American foreign policy. In fact, there had been several policy reactions to the concept of neutralism, ranging from the late John Foster Dulles' declaration of the "immorality of neutralism" to reluctant U.S. support of neutralism—but not as expounded by Sékou Touré. I must admit that Toure's emphasis on the humanitarian aspects of neutralism, which supposedly served the "highest interests of humanity" and favored the "right of self-determination," had little appeal to U.S. statesmen once they learned of the methods employed by Touré's Democratic Party of Guinea to render powerless Fulah chieftains in the domestic struggle for independence.

Had Touré really placed humanitarian motives above what he took to be the national interest, he would have experienced greater difficulty in obtaining independence for Guinea. He would have thought twice before giving even tacit approval to the use of coercion to force many Fulahs and their chieftains to vote for independence in the September 1958 Referendum. Touré might have reconciled himself to this situation by thinking that he was indeed serving the "interests of

humanity" by providing the rest of Africa with the example
of a developing nation following an independent policy. Undoubtedly, he felt that the success of the Guinean experiment
was going to enhance the dignity of all developing peoples and
reveal their possible future role on the international level.

At numerous times the Guinean policy of positive neutrality seemed to be somewhat opportunistic. But then there
was also the case of the late Indian leader Nehru, who in
countenancing armed intervention in Goa, seemingly dis-
carded neutralism when it was deemed necessary for the perceived national interest. However, Touré, in believing that
he could obtain economic aid from the West and the East,
might have reasoned that if he did so his country stood less
chance of losing its national sovereignty. He might have
thought that Guinean neutralism would serve to reduce
foreign influence by balancing the East and the West in
"compensatory dependence." Touré felt that his prestige
as a national and international leader would be enhanced
greatly if he could achieve several significant diplomatic
coups. These coups would enable him to postpone at home the
confrontation with pressing domestic problems. Unfortunately, Touré's plans for achieving diplomatic victories were
thwarted because the Russians made the mistakes of giving
useless aid and of intervening in internal affairs, while the
United States and other Western powers reacted much too
slowly.

I have always believed that Touré's radical stance stemmed
not only from his anticolonial bias, but also from his frustration at the fact that the much-talked-about East-West con-

271

frontation, with its usually predictable concomitant of extensive economic aid, never moved into high gear. Touré's bias and frustration made it easier for him to believe that American aid agreements always had *strings,* whereas the simpler agreements of Communist bloc countries did not have any *strings.* (It is interesting to note that British officials showed great flexibility and ingenuity in devising a simplified form of agreement that contrasted sharply with the more difficult form of the U.S. bilateral agreement.)

For a charismatic leader such as Sékou Touré, who during the period of transition appeared to be the only Guinean capable of unifying his country, a foreign policy based upon neutralism was of inestimable help in asserting the identity, integrity, and uniqueness of a new republic made up of different tribal groups. The more recognition he gained on the international scene while pursuing his "middle of the road" neutralism, the more this prestige enabled him to stifle on the domestic front any nascent opposition. Touré stressed incessantly at home and abroad the uniqueness of the Guinean experience and the importance of Guinean independence.

It is my belief that the Republic of Guinea served as a laboratory not only for Africa, but also for the West and the East. It revealed what can happen to an emerging nation when it is struggling to achieve stability and viability and is attempting, at the same time, to safeguard its sovereignty. There were valuable lessons to be drawn from the Guinean experience by the United States in particular, because of its large foreign aid program and its role of world leadership. The revamping of the Soviet aid approach in Guinea and the

272

rest of Africa was proof that the Soviet Union had learned from the Guinean experience. As far as France is concerned, it learned its lesson so well in Guinea that it did not experience similar problems with the remaining sub-Saharan African territories that sought independence soon afterwards. Indeed, France helped these nations become independent states and still managed to maintain economic, cultural, and social ties with them without incurring charges of "paternalism" or "neocolonialism."

Obviously, the neutralism practiced by the Republic of Guinea is not in the same tradition as the neutrality exemplified by Switzerland, in which a state, strong and independent of external support, has been able to play the role of "bystander" in international politics. It would be unrealistic to think that a country as economically and militarily weak as Guinea, and as dependent for its development on foreign aid, could play the role of arbiter or mediator in international politics. The recent unsuccessful efforts of Ghana and Guinea, as well as several other developing nations, to serve as mediator between the United States and Hanoi point up the questionable ability of neutralist nations to mediate international disputes.

Guinea impressed me always as being ready to take a stand somewhere between the East and the West on crucial issues in order to protect its imagined bargaining position. More often than not the Guinean stand was closer to that of the East than of the West. Nevertheless, I am unwilling to go quite as far as Dr. Henry Kissinger, who believes that neutralist countries will not assume substantial responsibilities in

273

coping with problems unrelated to their immediate interests. After all, Ghana and Guinea did offer to mediate in the crisis between North Vietnam and the United States. I do agree with Kissinger's belief that the tendency of neutralist countries to take a position somewhere between the contenders places a premium on Soviet intransigence. These countries have discovered that starting from extreme demands seems often to constitute profitable bargaining tactics. I admit also that any anticapitalist bias or any enlightened self-interest on the part of a neutralist country would place in question the ability of that country to serve justly as a mediator.

The whole question of the role of neutralist nations in international affairs presents a series of paradoxes, not the least of which is that the strength and safety of the stance of these nations depend upon the economic, political, and military strength of the United States. The ability of neutralist countries to serve as mediators depends upon the willingness of the West and the East to accept their mediation. The moment neutralist countries indicate a willingness to mediate, they bring upon themselves the pressures of the cold war which they claim they wish to avoid. These nations cannot remain truly uninvolved, because on certain issues, such as African problems, they are very definitely aligned on one side or the other. Under the present scheme of things, the neutralist Afro-Asian bloc is able at times to wield considerable voting power at the United Nations. Yet as soon as the UN discussions are ended, this same bloc has no real power to prevent unilateral action that might be taken by a dissenting great power.

The United States should have learned certain valuable lessons from its dealings with neutralist Guinea. For example, the State Department must never again be in the position of being without a sufficient number of Foreign Service officers who are knowledgeable in African affairs and African languages; the State Department must never again allow the problems of Africa to be settled largely in the Bureau of European Affairs rather than in the Bureau of African Affairs; the President, ably backstopped by an enlightened and efficient Secretary of State and State Department, must have the final say on policy. Furthermore, once it has been clearly established that the U.S. Chief of Mission in a foreign country has developed firm rapport with the President or Prime Minister, the members of the government, and the people, and has secured their confidence, the State Department should pay closer attention to the evaluations, policy suggestions, questions, requests, and advice of this Chief of Mission and his staff.

There were other lessons gained from U.S. contact with the Guinean situation, among which were at least two that proved invaluable in the subsequent reformulation of U.S. policy toward neutralist nations. The first lesson was simply that the United States must exert great care to avoid intervention or involvement in the internal affairs of the nations it seeks to aid. Perhaps we have followed this lesson closely in our dealings with countries other than Guinea, but I submit that the Soviet experience in Guinea clearly illustrated the danger of meddling in the internal affairs of a neutralist nation. Such meddling forced Guinea to turn in another direction to offset the continuing influence of the Soviet Union. The second lesson pointed up the importance of distributing aid not merely with the idea of combating Communist influence. Attempts to counterbalance Soviet political or economic influence by trying to swing the balance in our favor with aid deals have ended usually in our becoming more susceptible to "competitive blackmail" and to failure. Admittedly, the slogan of using foreign aid to win the battle over communism has been stressed in the past in order to get aid bills through the U.S. Congress; but this ploy for winning congressional support has also become part of the aid program itself.

Arthur Schlesinger, in describing Guinea's movement toward the Communist bloc countries in his recent book on the Kennedy administration, has stated incorrectly: "Touré even refused to receive Eisenhower's retiring ambassador for a farewell call." Schlesinger does give, however, an excellent summary of the fundamental changes effected in the U.S. foreign aid program under the Kennedy administration. It is very noticeable that even with the transition from the "country store" and "projects" approach of the old ICA to the new AID emphasis on long-range national planning, economic development, institutional and cultural growth, and "stronger national independence," neither the Kennedy administration nor the Johnson administration has settled the question of bilateral and multilateral aid.

Under the prevailing concept of bilateral aid, U.S. policymakers seemingly are sometimes put in the position of choosing between a "conciliatory" and a "discriminatory" policy.

They decide apparently on the basis of the international alignment or nonalignment of the nation aid recipient in question. When the policy makers are opponents of the aid policy, they declare it to be too "conciliatory" in that it provides aid for countries regardless of the degree of their neutrality. They contend that such a policy makes it easier for neutralist countries to support Communist bloc countries and still not have to fear the loss of U.S. aid; or they insist that this "conciliatory" policy encourages radical neutralism among nations that curry Soviet favor but do not wish to lose U.S. support altogether.

On the other hand, policy makers may maintain that the prevailing policy is too "discriminatory" if it seems to provide only for those countries adhering to less radical and biased neutralist policies. They then assert that a "discriminatory" policy does not necessarily encourage neutralist nations to take stands more favorable to the United States.

Whether the policy makers consider the aid policy "conciliatory" or "discriminatory," they are alike in wishing to be reassured that the policy is administered according to the needs of the country in question, its perceived alignment in international affairs, and its strategic importance to the United States.

It is not too farfetched to predict that as our policy makers become more and more troubled by the aid dilemma they are going to give more serious thought to channeling U.S. aid through international organizations such as the World Bank and the International Development Association. These organizations are recognized as having the expertise and the experience necessary to ensure that unjustifiable economic projects will not be approved. Some members of Congress will not be happy at the prospect of using international organizations for aid purposes, because they do not wish to see the United States become so uninvolved that it can no longer exert control over where and how aid funds are to be placed. Despite the expressed agreement of former Aid Director David Bell with the desirability of a multilateral approach for U.S. aid, the Johnson administration has shown little inclination to move in this direction. The Johnson administration might be willing to give more support to a multilateral approach if other countries involved in administering aid were to indicate a willingness to make more use of international organizations.

I never lost the conviction during my stay in Guinea that America, because of its well-known policy of promoting self-determination for nations and its respect for the sovereignty of independent nations, had an important role to play in safeguarding Guinea's sovereignty. I regretted very much that our policy makers were deceived initially in their efforts to reach an estimate of Sékou Touré and his Government by reports emanating from French sources. I am not trying to say that when Sékou Touré rejected Communist social ideas he rejected also the economic and political ideas which his Marxist orientation caused him to believe could be adapted to the African communal way of life. But when Touré discovered that much of the Russian machinery was unsuited for Guinea's purposes, and realized that showcase enterprises were not helping the Guinean economy, was it correct to believe that he had become disillusioned? It was more likely that Touré was disgusted and disappointed to find his country saddled with useless machinery. Was Touré really disillusioned when he found out how much the Russians had become involved in Guinean internal affairs—an involvement resulting from a false Soviet estimate of the bloc hold on Guinea? One thing is certain: Touré was thoroughly enraged and ready to take instant action.

It seems to me that disillusionment implies a previous willingness on the part of Touré to place his trust and his fate in the hands of the Communists. Is it not true, however, that Touré's previous dependence on the Communist bloc countries was due partially to a lack of available alternate sources? Of course, Touré might have been more disposed to depend upon the bloc because of his anticolonialist and anti-imperialist point of view. The fact remains, however, that when he was in deep trouble the first nation to which he turned for modest help was the United States. Did the United States answer this distress signal? Is it possible that what appeared to be an intentional submission to the Communist bloc countries which led inevitably to economic dependence upon bloc aid was nothing more than a hastily improvised "middle of the road" policy devised by inexperienced and bewildered leaders?

It is difficult to say whether or not Touré trusted the Communists and was therefore disillusioned by their perfidy. He never struck me as being naïve, and he was certainly very realistic and tough-minded. If he had believed that the Communists would help him and would not attempt to subvert and overthrow his Government, then he might have been a disillusioned leader. But if he remained ever alert to the possibilities of subversion—and he did react quickly and vigorously to stop demonstrations in 1961 and also expelled the Soviet Ambassador—then he was not disillusioned.

Touré's constant awareness of his precarious position on the international scene—and today, perhaps, on the local scene—and his previous exclusion of any African Communist party from the Guinean political arena seem to indicate that he was a wary individual. Indeed, those who were aware of this quality in Touré were among the first to reject the erroneous reports spread in world capitals in March 1966 concerning his stepping down and turning the presidency of Guinea over to the deposed Ghanaian leader, Kwame Nkrumah. Those who had some knowledge of Touré's way of thinking and acting recognized that Touré had bestowed upon Nkrumah nothing more than an "honorific presidency." It was inconceivable that the Guinean leader, after eight years of struggle to retain the leadership of his country, would hand over the reins to a non-French-speaking former rival.

I have pointed out before my vain efforts to convince Washington officials between 1959 and 1961 that Sékou Touré was an African nationalist who was struggling to maintain and preserve Guinean independence and merited receiving U.S. support. It was very fortunate, therefore, for the future U.S. position in Africa that President Kennedy had the foresight, wisdom, and courage to believe in 1961 that Touré was a nationalist. It was fortunate also that he instructed his diplomatic representative to Guinea, Ambassador William Attwood, to verify his feeling about the Guinean leader. Attwood confirmed Kennedy's conviction about Touré, and Kennedy and Attwood decided upon a course of action in Guinea that made it clear that the United States stood ready to recognize genuine nonalignment.

Recalling how Touré tried to imply that the United States and Kennedy were in some fashion responsible for the death of Patrice Lumumba, and how the Guinean President not only accepted the Lenin Peace Prize, but also publicly affirmed his total support for Castro after the Bay of Pigs incident, Arthur Schlesinger remarks:

> Despite all this, Kennedy felt that Sékou Touré remained a nationalist at heart; and, before William Attwood departed as his ambassador to Conakry, the President asked him to verify this as best he could.
>
> Attwood found the American position less hopeless than it seemed from Washington. The Russian aid program, it turned out, was a great mess. The materials were poor, the technicians officious and incompetent, the diplomats insistent and patronizing. Returning to Washington in May, Attwood reported a slow disillusionment and recommended a small American aid program to show Sékou Touré that the United States was willing to go along with genuine non-alignment. Outside the Bureau of African Affairs, the bureaucracy regarded this with disdain as another gust of New Frontier naïveté. Then Robert Kennedy came back from the Ivory Coast and vigorously backed Attwood.
>
> . . . By the spring of 1962, American aid was beginning to arrive. . . . And, when Touré came to New York in October for the UN General Assembly, the President asked him down to Washington. Kennedy met him at the airport and took him back to the White House, where they talked over the problems

of Guinea for an hour in the Cabinet Room. Then Kennedy brought him over to the Mansion, introduced him to Jacqueline and Caroline and gave him a formal luncheon.

. . . From this time on Touré felt that he had a friend at the White House and sent personal messages at the slightest pretext.

The Attwood-Kennedy policy was able to succeed, of course, because it came at the right time. But, if Washington had persisted in its conviction that Guinea was irreclaimable, we would not have been in the position to take advantage of the Soviet errors.

We must stop paying mere lip service to the idea of self-determination for nations and the development of states that are politically independent and economically viable. We must re-examine our policy of containment and stop giving African nations the impression that our interest in them is determined solely by cold-war considerations. We must avoid the appearance of ignoring those nations which are consistently friendly toward us and of rewarding those nations that flout the things for which we stand. We must convince African nations that our African policy is a consistent one, not something made from day to day as we move from one crisis to another. And we must hold up alternatives for these African states other than their having to remain dependent upon their former colonial administrators or being forced to move into the back yards of the Soviet or Chinese Communists. The thought which I have in mind is much better expressed by Dr. Arnold Rivkin, who asserts:

> The United States must redress the imbalance in its foreign policies by refocusing its view of American interests in Africa,

282

not by downgrading our traditional interest in Europe or by denying the reality of the cold war, but rather by upgrading the importance of Africa, formulating policies responsive to African realities and striking a reasonable balance among our multiple interests. The United States needs to rationalize its political and economic policies in Africa, to make them consistent and credible and thus responsive to our national interest in the development of stable and viable African states.

Not only from the people of Guinea but also from the people of other developing nations of Africa, I learned of their great desire for immediate change and their earnest hope to have all of the appurtenances of modern civilization, including such projects as the Konkouré and Volta Dams. I sensed that fresh in their memories were the unfavorable consequences of colonialism which had made use of racial and social discrimination, and I knew that they little appreciated being reminded that they were trying to accomplish in an incredibly short time what some nations had taken several centuries to achieve. But to me, most remarkable of all was the fact that these people still held the belief that the United States remained the land of the "original anticolonial people." This belief persisted despite the adverse publicity abroad about the American race problem.

There are indications that the Johnson administration might consider sanctioning U.S. involvement in an effort to draw up a "vast economic program" for emerging African nations, with the idea of creating eventually an African Common Market. It is not perhaps too optimistic to hope that the idea of creating an African Common Market might have some chance of becoming a reality, with the recent entrance on the scene of a new crop of African leaders with a new orientation. (The removal of Nkrumah in Ghana in March 1966 marked the sixth coup in Africa within a four-month period.) Whatever may happen, I trust sincerely that the Johnson administration is going to make a more concerted effort in the very near future to develop an effective and dynamic U.S. policy in Africa. I hope also that in this era of African independence we shall not grow weary and allow our great nation to shirk its responsibilities of world leadership.

INDEX